# Activating the Primary Social Studies Classroom

## *A Standards-Based Sourcebook for K–4*

Leslie Marlow and Duane Inman

ScarecrowEducation
Lanham, Maryland • Toronto • Oxford
2005

Published in the United States of America
by ScarecrowEducation
An imprint of The Rowman & Littlefield Publishing Group, Inc.
4501 Forbes Boulevard, Suite 200, Lanham, Maryland 20706
www.scarecroweducation.com

PO Box 317
Oxford
OX2 9RU, UK

British Library Cataloguing in Publication Information Available

**Library of Congress Cataloging-in-Publication Data**

Marlow, Leslie, 1956–
  Activating the primary social studies classroom : a standards-based
sourcebook for K–4 / Leslie Marlow and Duane Inman.
     p. cm.
  Includes bibliographical references and index.
  ISBN 1-57886-241-8 (pbk. : alk. paper)
  1. Social sciences—Study and teaching (Primary)—Activity programs—
United States. 2. Interdisciplinary approach in education—United States.
3. Education, Primary—Aims and objectives—United States. I. Inman,
Duane, 1945– . II. Title.
LB1530.M38 2005
372.83—dc22

                                                                    2004027007

To Swafford and Frank

# Contents

# *Preface*

In order to be effective, educators must present social studies as a dynamic, active, and interactive process, one through which students are required to think about relationships, interpret events, and conduct inquiry that will assist them in making informed decisions in contemporary life. Becoming actively involved in content-related activities provides students with a unique way of familiarizing themselves with the present, empowering them to know where they are in time and where they have come from so the past becomes more than a series of stories. Information about the past must be combined with current events and plans for the future to enable students to make contemporary decisions based to some degree on what has gone before, on knowledge of actual experiences, and on best predictions of what may occur in the future.

As has been adequately demonstrated and documented throughout the history of education, students can easily memorize material. But memorization of facts is a mechanical process, not only extremely boring but also of limited use and duration. In order to make social studies meaningful, real questions must be proposed that will appeal to students' natural curiosity. Students need to be "captured" by the personal relevance of information. The lure is the comedy and tragedy of events, the personalities involved, and the outcomes—both good and bad—of various social studies topics. Social studies stories can be enacted through multidisciplinary activities that enable students to participate in simulated events; vicariously make decisions similar to ones made before or ones that have never been made; and compare and contrast events, people, places, and decisions related to a variety of cultures.

## ORGANIZATION OF MATERIALS

This book promotes activity-oriented studies for grades K–4 that are linked with each of the standards of the National Council for the Social Studies. These activities are designed to promote learning in a global society. Important features include:

- Adaptable activities within the various areas of the social sciences and with integration of children's literature, using social studies as the content area vehicle through which all other subjects can be taught
- "User-friendly" content activities that can easily be conducted using low-cost materials to which most teachers have easy access
- Focus on fewer worksheet activities
- Emphasis on encouraging students to be totally immersed in activities that require them to think in creative and critical ways, to solve problems, and to make decisions as they construct knowledge

The introduction provides information related to the definition of social studies, the disciplines that comprise social studies, and the ten social studies standards identified by the National Council for the Social Studies (NCSS). It also contains a short list of social studies terms.

Chapters 1–10 are organized according to each of the ten NCSS standards. Information that describes the components of each standard precedes each set of activities. Each chapter includes the use of specific children's literature to accompany the activities. Technological resources related to the topic are located at the end of each activity. Suggestions for accommodations and extensions of the activities are also included. The source of many of the quotes used at the beginning of the introductory section in each of these chapters is the Famous Quotations Network, located at www.famousquotations.com/acategories.asp.

The appendixes provide additional resources: background information for several activities in the book, names and addresses of professional organizations that can provide information related to social studies content and content integration, names and addresses of professional periodicals for teachers and magazines for children, and information on assessment and evaluation instruments that can be used with the activities in the book.

## SPECIAL FEATURES

Within each chapter, the activities are organized according to the following format:

1. A summary and objective for the activity is located at the beginning of the activity immediately following the activity title.
2. Listed immediately below the objective is basic information such as the amount of time needed for the activity, group size, process skills addressed, social studies disciplines addressed, other content areas addressed, key vocabulary, and a listing of materials needed to accomplish the activity.
3. Detailed procedures for conducting the activity follow. Lessons that have multiple components are divided into various parts.
4. The adaptations and accommodations section provides ways to change or extend the activity so it will cover additional content, be appropriate for a lower grade, or be appropriate for a higher grade.
5. A listing of children's books to use with the topic is organized alphabetically by author.
6. An annotated set of technology resources for use with students or for use as a teacher resource is located at the end of each activity.

## ACKNOWLEDGMENTS

We would like to acknowledge the significant contributions that were made during the development of this text: the last 15 years' worth of graduate and undergraduate students, pre-service teachers, and in-service teachers who contributed ideas, feedback, and thoughtful discussions on new and innovative ideas and the individuals and professional organizations who provided their expertise and content knowledge.

We would also like to express our gratitude to the reviewers who so thoughtfully read and offered suggestions to the work in progress.

# Introduction
## Social Studies and the National Standards

The difficulty many teachers experience in defining social studies compels them to use the standard definition of social studies developed by the National Council for the Social Studies (NCSS) in 1992. An examination of the various components of the definition provides evidence of the inclusiveness of the social studies curriculum.

"Social studies is the integrated study of the social sciences and humanities to promote civic competence." This first portion of the NCSS definition emphasizes at least two very important components. The first phrase, "the integrated study," indicates there is no one aspect, topic, or subject that encompasses social studies. Rather, social studies is a compilation of materials, skills, behaviors, resources, and content that comprises the second area of importance, "civic competence." Consequently, according to the initial portion of the NCSS definition, social studies is, by design, supposed to integrate a wide variety of skills and content that enable people to become competent citizens in society.

The NCSS definition then continues as follows:

Within the school program, social studies provides coordinated, systematic study drawing upon such disciplines as anthropology, archaeology, economics, geography, history, law, philosophy, political science, psychology, religion, and sociology as well as appropriate content from the humanities, mathematics, and natural sciences.

This inclusiveness provides educators with an extremely wide array of topics through which to encourage the development of civic competence:

| Discipline | The study of |
| --- | --- |
| anthropology | humankind |
| archaeology | human culture |
| ecology | interrelationships of organisms and their environment |
| economics | goods and services |
| geography | earth and life distribution |
| history | the past |
| law | rules, customs, and practices |
| philosophy | ways of thinking and approaching life |
| political science | government |
| psychology | human behavior |
| religion | beliefs and theology of the world |
| sociology | societies of the world |

The number and diversity of the areas, by their very nature, provide opportunities for students to work and acquire knowledge and experiences in areas applicable to them. Connections between past and contemporary issues can be established. Teachers can avoid following the simple requirement that students memorize information that may or may not apply to society as it is today.

The final line of the NCSS definition focuses on the primary purpose of social studies: "To help young people develop the ability to make informed and reasoned decisions for the public good as citizens of a culturally diverse, democratic society in an interdependent world." This implies the need for students to develop the skills and acquire the knowledge necessary to think creatively and critically, to become problem solvers, and to make decisions, all based on their knowledge of the diverse society in which they live.

## TEN STRANDS OF THE NCSS STANDARDS

The standards and position statements developed by NCSS (1994) identify ten areas, or strands, that should be included in the social studies curriculum. All social studies programs, particularly when they are part of an integrated curriculum, must include activities and experiences that provide examination and knowledge acquisition in these areas. The ten strands are as follows: (1) Culture; (2) Time, Continuity, and Change; (3) People, Places, and Environments; (4) Individual Development and Identity; (5) Individuals, Groups, and Institutions; (6) Power, Authority, and Governance; (7) Production, Distribution, and Consumption; (8) Science, Technology, and Society; (9) Global Connections; and (10) Civic Ideals and Practices. Following is a brief description of each strand and the key disciplines (as found in the definition of social studies) to which each strand relates.

## Culture

Since all cultures exhibit similarities and differences in such areas as folktales, traditions, education, folkways, and mores, students should compare and contrast cultural perspectives so they can relate to various people around the world. In the early grades, as students begin to interact with others, exploration of likenesses and differences is an appropriate introduction into cultural diversity. As students reach the middle grades, the nature of culture, as well as specific cultural differences and similarities, should be explored. Students must be provided opportunities to discover how language, music, and art express culture and how they influence and are influenced by people's behavior.

Key disciplines include anthropology, geography, and history.

## Time, Continuity, and Change

The study of the past, present, and future, and the ways in which they are linked, provides students with insights into how we see ourselves throughout time. Primarily as part of history, younger students enjoy hearing stories from the past, particularly those related to people, places, and things they know, and learning how the past impacts the present. This provides the foundation for later learning, when students begin to study specific historical events and expand their understanding of the past and of differing historical perspectives. Opportunities should be provided for students to demonstrate understanding of how particular incidents can be interpreted and described in alternative ways.

Key disciplines include history and the humanities.

## People, Places, and Environments

Studying people, places, and environments can assist students in creating their perspectives on various areas of the world. By examining how these three aspects relate, interact, and are dependent on one another, students begin to make reasoned, informed decisions about living things and their environment. Personal experiences provide the basis for this information in the earlier grades, with the focus becoming more global and vicarious in the middle grades. Maps, globes, and photographs should be used so that students can create, interpret, use, and distinguish information about changes in people, places, and environments over time.

Key disciplines include geography and ecology.

## Individual Development and Identity

As students explore how one's identity is shaped by other individuals, as well as by one's culture, organizations, and institutions, they begin to gain knowledge about society's expectations, values, and standards. In turn, this knowledge enhances understanding of how one grows as an individual. In the early grades, students begin to develop their identities in the context of siblings, parents, and communities. As they grow older, peers play a more prominent role in shaping identity, and students begin to examine their own beliefs in relation to those of their peers and others within their culture. Unique features of families and the ways ethnic, regional, and global cultures influence their lives on a daily basis must be examined to promote understanding of one's self and others. This understanding enables the individual to appreciate the motivation, thought processes, and actions of others both similar to and different from themselves.

Key disciplines include anthropology and psychology.

## Individuals, Groups, and Institutions

Because of the influence institutions such as church, school, governmental agencies, and social groups have on the individual, it is necessary for students to be aware of how institutions are formed, who influences and maintains or changes them, and how institutions influence or control the individual. Young learners must be given opportunities to explore and discuss how various institutions influence them personally. This learning will lead to the middle-level topics of how institutions change over time, how they influence conformity or nonconformity, and how they influence social norms. Identifying the roles students play in situations related to families or groups should be stressed.

Key disciplines include anthropology, history, political science, psychology, and sociology.

## Power, Authority, and Governance

To develop civic competence, students must engage in activities that promote understanding the development of structures of power, authority, and governance within their own country as well as within other countries. Whereas fairness, rules, authority, and guidelines play a large part in teaching students in the early grades about governance issues, middle-grade students can focus more on how personal rights and responsibilities impact local, state, regional, and national issues. The focus must be on the purpose of government when teaching civic competence related to power, authority, and governance.

Key disciplines include government, history, law, and political science.

## Production, Distribution, and Consumption

Four primary issues are addressed in primary-grade classrooms in relation to production, distribution, and consumption: What goods and services should be produced? How should they be produced? How should they be distributed? and What is the most effective allocation method of the goods, services, and their production factors? Young students can distinguish between wants and needs as well as between goods and services, and they can begin to identify personal economic experiences related to their communities. In the middle grades, students should expand the basic knowledge from the earlier grades and make applications related to state, regional, national, and global situations. Being able to define and identify examples of these aspects of production, distribution, and consumption should be combined with opportunities to comprehend related items in current events. Concepts of personal and governmental budgeting should be stressed.

The key discipline is economics.

### Science, Technology, and Society

Science and technology impact society over time and in the process change lives globally. Young students can study how technology and science have worked together to invent many things we currently have in our lives as well as things that have been replaced by newer inventions. In the middle grades, students should explore how science, technology, and society impact human behavior, values, and quality of life. Current trends of technological and scientific growth should be explored. The relationships among these three items, rather than the study of each independently, should be the focus of this strand.

Key disciplines include economics, geography, government, and history, as well as the natural and physical sciences and the humanities.

### Global Connections

Understanding global connections is related to many areas—environment, human rights, economics, and political science, to name but a few. Often in the context of current events, students must be provided with multiple opportunities to examine and analyze relationships among and between cultures of the world. In the younger grades, use of newspapers and television news items can provide exposure to specific issues and concerns around the world. In the middle grades, analysis of these types of media stories can be implemented. In all instances the focus should be on the role of the individual within the global community.

Key disciplines include economics and geography as well as the natural and physical sciences and the humanities.

## Civic Ideals and Practices

To be fully competent functional members of society, people must understand the need to positively participate in citizenship practices. Additionally, they must be able to make connections among the ideals on which a given society is founded, their personal beliefs, and current practices in society related to rights, responsibilities, and a citizen's role in a community, state, nation, and the world. In the early grades, allowing students to help set classroom guidelines and expectations, while discussing the roles of the individual and the whole group as part of these guidelines and expectations, serves to introduce students to their roles in one particular community. As students move into the middle grades, these classroom experiences should be expanded, and parallels should be drawn to communities outside the classroom. Primarily, students need opportunities to examine themselves and their roles in relation to others in any type of community.

Key disciplines include anthropology, government, history, and political science.

# THE SOCIAL STUDIES TEACHING ENVIRONMENT

## Adaptations/Accommodations of the Learning Environment

Adaptation must occur in social studies to modify lessons for individual students so the unique abilities of each student are met. As students learn how to learn, their behavior will change as their number of learning strategies increases. To enable students to learn and accomplish more, numerous models and strategies must be used, but adaptations and modifications must also be made so all students can learn at ever-higher levels of proficiency.

## Basic Teaching Assumptions

**Assumption One.** "Students will be able to work together cooperatively." Knowledge and understanding are derived in a social setting according to constructivist theory. In life, people must constantly be able to adapt to various situations and to the expectations of other people if they are to succeed in today's and tomorrow's global community. Therefore, it is not unrealistic to expect students to work in a cooperative environment and exhibit social adaptability.

**Assumption Two.** "Students will be able to best learn content through active involvement." In cooperative settings, learners are exposed to verbal, auditory, kinesthetic, inter-personal, and intrapersonal stimuli in conjunction with logical/mathematical, artistic, musical, or naturalistic experiences. Folk wisdom attributed to Confucius says, "Tell me, and I forget. Show me, and I remember. Let me do, and I understand." A more Western and contemporary version is, "Give a man a fish, and you feed him for a day. Teach a man to fish, and you feed him for a lifetime."

**Assumption Three.** "Students will be able to take responsibility for their own learning." Opportunities can be presented to students, but the individual student decides whether or not and to what degree he or she will take advantage of these opportunities. This philosophy, known as control theory, recognizes that learning cannot be forced on anyone. Ultimately, each member of society must accept responsibility for his or her own actions. The school environment must provide a safe place in which to learn this essential approach to successful living.

**Assumption Four.** "Students will be able to construct meaning as they work through their own cognitive processes." Meaning is highly personal. When students construct knowledge from within their own schemata, they are engaged in active learning. As cognition occurs within, the very act of thinking fosters change in the individual. Working toward meaning within a constructivist environment enables students to become lifelong learners who construct new meaning from and for the dynamic society in which they live.

**Assumption Five.** "Students will be able to take ownership as they control their own learning." Ownership implies there is something of value to be owned. For almost all humans, that which the individual creates, the individual values. Ownership of knowledge, ideas, and thoughts can become a powerful possession. It is often said that we are living in the "age of information." If information or knowledge is something we value as a commodity, if it forms the raw material for our social fabric, then ownership of knowledge becomes valuable and desirable. Ownership of *new* knowledge, one's *own* knowledge, becomes a powerful motivating factor.

## Coach/Facilitator

The coach/facilitator instructional strategy allows the teacher to provide an environment supportive of the students' endeavors. While actively monitoring students, walking among the various groups or individuals engaged in tasks, the teacher directs student inquiry by asking higher-order questions. While it is important for the coach/facilitator to provide positive reinforcement and motivational statements as the students work, the primary job of the teacher in this model is to encourage students to engage in learning experiences beyond what may be readily apparent. Information and responses to direct student questions are addressed by assisting student inquiry into appropriate resources.

## Constructivism

Constructivism is an approach to learning that places the learner's physical and cognitive activities at the central focus of the learning process. Constructivism encourages individual students to make linkages within their range of experiences with new concepts, facts, and ideas and to make practical applications of their new knowledge outside of school.

## Content Integration

Content integration involves explicit overlap of content from different subjects as part of teacher-constructed thematic units or of student-directed cross-subject projects, such as in the Wagon Westward Ho! activity (chapter 2). Children's literature, as well as a variety of print and nonprint media, is drawn upon as part of content integration, particularly in the social studies. Application of math, science, language arts, and the humanities occurs within the selected social studies topics so that instructional activities meet the major objectives identified for each discipline.

## Cooperative Learning

Cooperative learning occurs in environments that promote active student engagement while students work collaboratively within small groups, generally of three to five students. Collaborative groups can be composed of students in ability groupings, interest groupings, multiage groupings, or multigrade groupings. Each person within the group has a job, as demonstrated in the Trip activity (chapter 9). Teamwork among the group members becomes both part of the strategy and a goal of this approach. Cooperative learning activities emphasize the acceptance of differences, the value of each person's contributions, and the importance of assisting and supporting other members of the group as students learn to work cooperatively. Ways in which to adapt cooperative groups include the following:

- Allowing a wide range of ability levels within each group and assigning mixed-ability groups. This allows each member of the group to work on one aspect of the assignment at his or her particular skill level and ability.
- Assigning only one set of materials per group. Without duplicates of needed materials, group members must learn to collaborate and share.
- Identifying specific roles for individuals within the group. Additionally, varying the assigned roles so all students can attempt all roles with peer assistance available.
- Allowing partial participation within groups. If certain individuals are not able to fully participate for any reason, social interaction and modeling within the group will still be beneficial.

## Direct Instruction

A teacher-focused model of instruction that uses a teacher-directed lecture to first provide the academic focus for the class is referred to as direct instruction. As an entire group, the class listens to information put forth by the teacher and responds to pointed questions when asked. However, use of direct instruction should be only one part of the total teaching package. Immediately following direct instruction, the teacher should move students beyond the content-knowledge level and into higher-order personal learning by engaging them in student-directed or shared teacher/student-directed activities, such as the Crime Solving activity (chapter 8). The outcome is that each student will apply the content knowledge within the context of his or her own environment and experiences, thereby personalizing information and making abstract concepts individually meaningful.

## Environments

For social studies teaching to be most conducive to learning, the educational environment must provide a variety of activities, including large-group instruction, small-group instruction, discussion, learning centers, and independent work during the course of the day. This variety of instructional models demands a variety of learning environment arrangements. A teacher who encourages responses to activities that address visual, auditory, and kinesthetic learning will eliminate the boredom that naturally and inevitably occurs when the same type of activity or assignment is done repeatedly. Other adaptations for the environment include the following:

- Providing activities and unstructured time that allow for physical movement. Large motor skills, as well as fine motor skills, need to be used. Allowing students to take short breaks from work and to move around within or outside the classroom, including socialization time, also keeps boredom at bay and directs energy into productive rather than destructive activities.
- Providing in the room a written schedule, directions, or a checklist to which students can refer to assist with their personal organization and time management. Reading the information aloud as transition time occurs allows auditory and visual learners to focus on what is to happen next. Allowing students to have a duplicate of the daily schedule also allows kinesthetic learners to go through the process of checking off items as they progress through the day.
- Providing seating that matches students' needs to specific locations. Temperature, location, light sensitivity, socialization patterns, and the

like all impact student learning and should be taken into consideration each day. Movement of seating around the room on a daily or weekly basis, keeping individual needs in mind, will also help students begin to feel comfortable in a variety of settings.

## Experiential Learning

Experiential learning emphasizes hands-on, manipulative activities performed by students, as in the Rally activity (chapter 3). Using manipulatives, resources, simulations, and learning centers in which active participation occurs defines the essence of experiential learning. Inquiry and discovery learning often comprise a component of the experiential learning strategy. In both, the teacher acts as facilitator while students, independently or in groups, work to gather facts, answer questions, or determine outcomes that will be discussed in the classroom environment. With inquiry learning, the topic is decided on by students independently or by the whole class, whereas the topic for discovery learning is decided on by the teacher.

## Handouts and Worksheets

Worksheets and handouts should provide guided and independent practice of a concept or skill that has already been taught. For example, when learning about specific ancient civilizations, an appropriate worksheet, such as an Information Retrieval Chart (chapter 8) should be used. It is most important that worksheets and handouts not be used to teach the concept but rather to reinforce and provide a resource to which students can refer as they continue their learning. Handout and worksheet adaptations can include the following elements:

- Use clear, concise directions and, if possible, include a sample with the directions. Any information not absolutely necessary to the directions should be eliminated so students do not become confused.
- Avoid cluttered pages by using a lot of spacing on the page. Be sure there is adequate space in which to respond to questions, illustrate details, or list items. More space tends to be less threatening to students, as does larger print.

- Break worksheet or handout sections into boxes, or separate them with illustrations. By organizing each page in this way, students can look for cues that indicate a transition from one type of activity to the next. Additionally, try highlighting or placing an asterisk beside items that are particularly important.

## Independent Learning

Worksheets and "busy work" do not automatically constitute independent-learning opportunities. Students should be encouraged to work independently, focusing on student-centered projects or application of direct-instruction content. For example, concentrating on application activities as part of independent practice through construction of a Kamishibai Story (chapter 9) allows the teacher to determine if the content knowledge can be applied in a way unique and personal to individual students. The self-paced nature of independent learning allows students to work in their comfort zones, allowing each individual time to reflect upon his or her work and relate the findings to personal growth.

## Instruction

Social studies instruction should use a multisensory approach that focuses on all three modalities of learning: visual, auditory, and kinesthetic. The various models of instruction can be modified through any of the previously mentioned suggestions related to environment, cooperative learning, worksheets and handouts, and written assignments, as well as through the following:

- Providing several options (oral report, diagrams, artwork, etc.) for demonstrating knowledge on a particular topic.
- Avoiding placing students in competitive situations.
- Allowing extra in-class time for work completion.
- Paraphrasing information and encouraging students to repeat, summarize, and reexplain to one another.
- Expecting the same curriculum-content application from all students, but at differing grade levels depending on ability.

- Increasing response time following questions to allow students an opportunity to think before answering.
- Prerecording stories and reading assignments and allowing students to listen to the tapes.
- Using read-along tapes.
- Allowing students to read in pairs.

As teachers adapt social studies content, materials, and environment, the goal is to influence students' progress in such a manner that they become more flexible thinkers, add a variety of learning strategies to their collection, enjoy learning, and become successful. Increasing or decreasing the classroom structure to fit the level at which each student works best will ensure that social studies learning becomes a positive experience.

## Instructional Feedback

This method of instruction is similar to the coach/facilitator model. As with the coach/facilitator strategy, the teacher's purpose is to provide a supportive environment while actively monitoring groups and individuals. However, whereas the coach/facilitator strategy is orally conducted, instructional feedback can also occur in written form. Additionally, as the teacher monitors activities, such as with the Stop The Spies! activity (chapter 7), he or she can provide instructional feedback in the form of direct answers to students' questions or by providing general factual information to students.

## Models of Instruction

Instructional strategies that can be varied and used as part of the social studies curriculum are generally referred to as models of instruction. Models of instruction are typically divided into three groups: models with students as the primary focus, models with teachers as the primary focus, and models in which students and teachers are active participants in the process. Student-focused models of instruction include the following: coach/facilitator, instructional feedback, cooperative learning, experiential learning, and independent seat work.

## Process Skills

The six primary process skills are observing, classifying, measuring, communicating, inferring, and predicting. Other process skills such as hypothesizing, experimenting, analyzing, evaluating, and interpreting are combinations or extensions of the six primary process skills. These skills encourage use of higher-order questioning skills, with teachers and students involved in forming and responding to questions. Use of the process skills encourages students to ask why things occur, not to just simply know they occur. In asking why, students operate at higher levels of Bloom's taxonomy, especially in the development of analytical skills, evaluation skills, and the ability to synthesize new information and concepts from existing knowledge. Process-skill use leads to open-ended questions of "what would happen if . . . , or what would have happened if . . . ?"—an especially useful question when focusing on social studies topics.

## Student Discussion

For student discussion opportunities to be most effective, planning by the teacher should occur first, with the teacher identifying a set of initial questions about a particular topic, reading, or activity. From the initial set of questions, additional questions are generated by students and teacher, and discussion continues until the topic has been exhausted, such as in the Challenge of Belonging activity (chapter 1). The questions should be higher order, asking for more than just simple responses or basic recall. Additionally, the teacher and students must collaboratively construct a set of classroom guidelines by which to abide during the use of the student discussion strategy.

## Technology Use

The inclusion of technology in the social studies curriculum emphasizes the application of software and hardware as tools or resources by students and teacher as well as teacher-delivered instruction through the medium of various hardware and software. Technology use can easily permeate all other models of teaching and learning and can be used in individualized settings as well as with entire classes. Two primary uses of technology in the social studies curriculum include virtual field trips and the use of the Internet for research, enhancement, and activities.

## Written Assignments

In order to be purposeful, written assignments must allow learners ample opportunity to absorb the information being written and to reflect upon the information in order to make connections in the editing and revising process. Writing assignments and handwriting assignments should be taught as two separate items, thus allowing social studies content, rather than letter formation, spacing, and letter transitions, to be the focus of a writing assignment. In social studies, students can create interactive response cards as a group, thus writing information related to the topic in a way that reduces the amount of writing any one person is required to complete. While reducing paper and pencil tasks is the primary way to adapt written assignments, other possibilities are included below:

- Not always penalizing for spelling, punctuation, and grammar errors. If the purpose of the assignment is related to "what" is being written rather than "how" it is written, lack of penalization for these items will enhance the writing self-esteem of the individual.
- Allowing students to respond to items on a tape recorder or to classroom aides, peers, or other classroom assistants. While writing is an important aspect of the social studies curriculum, not all assignments must be responded to in writing.
- Not returning handwritten work to be rewritten. Chances are that the second version may not be any better than the first, and the rewriting causes increased frustration and lowered self-esteem.
- Pairing students for writing assignments. Two heads are said to be better than one, so it stands to reason that two people writing will be able to generate a higher-quality product in possibly less time.
- Conducting group interactive writing projects as part of guided practice with the teacher. With the entire group working together, many more ideas will be generated, and good modeling for writing will be produced.

# CHAPTER 1

# *Culture*

If you live on this land, and you have ancestors sleeping in this land, I believe that makes you a native to this land. It has nothing to do with the color of your skin. . . . We share a common root, and the root is Mother Earth.

—Oh Shinnah

Culture is defined as the complex interaction among the folkways, mores, and familial structures of a group of people, combined with the interactions of these components with the physical and biotic environments about them. Integrating the study of culture in the curriculum seeks to ensure that students develop an awareness of differences and similarities between their cultural backgrounds and those of others in an open and nonjudgmental manner. Additionally, it helps students develop understanding and affirmation of their own and others' unique cultural practices and heritages. Encouraged reflection on how their backgrounds may impact their relationships with people of diverse cultures will assist the development of students' approach to life in the emerging global community they will inherit.

In the lower grades, as students begin to interact with others, development of skills needed to achieve harmonious relationships between minority and mainstream cultural groups and exploration of likenesses and differences between these groups are appropriate introductions to cultural diversity. Focusing on places and regions provides a starting place for gaining information on the identities and lives of people. Opportunities must ultimately provide students with the abilities to identify human and physical characteristics of places, to explore the creation of regions in an attempt to interpret the complexity of life on earth, and to analyze people's perceptions of places and regions through cultures and experiences. The disciplines of anthropology, geography, and history provide connections for exploration in the lower grades.

## WHAT IS CULTURE?

Students explore the concept of culture through observation of items representing distinct elements of various cultures and discussion of cultural characteristics.

> Duration: 1–2 class periods
> Group Size: whole group
> Disciplines: language arts, fine arts
> Skills: describing, deducing, generalizing, analyzing, inferring
> Key Vocabulary: culture, cultural, stereotype, environment
> Materials: crayons, markers, chart paper, groups of objects representing different cultures (one from personal culture, others from other cultures—for example, food, native dress, pictures of homes, photographs of government buildings, religious icons, music)

**Procedure**

1. Show students culturally representative objects from your culture that you have brought from your home. Ask students to make generalizations about what they might know about you based on these objects. Record their responses on a chart.
2. Discuss that these responses are a method by which your culture is being described. Ask "What is culture?" Guide the discussion to help students form an awareness that culture describes the way in which a particular group of people lives. Included in culture are languages, dress, food, religion, celebrations, as well as other aspects of their lives. Discuss how these things affect, and are affected by, the physical environment. Discuss that people learn their culture primarily from parents and from other members of their family plus others in their community.

3. Show the objects from one of the other cultures. Discuss the way the people represented by these objects might live and how it differs from the one previously discussed. Repeat with cultural objects from other groups.
4. Discuss the following concepts: (a) cultures are different from one another, but none is better than another and (b) difficulties envisioned in joining a culture that is different from the one in which you grew up.
5. Read the book *Wake Up, World: A Day in the Life of Children around the World*. Discuss similarities and differences among children in the story.

## Extensions/Adaptations

- Use other books and have students identify ways in which the environments in the books differ from or are similar to those of the students.
- Have students bring items or photographs from home that represent their culture. Discuss similarities and differences in class.
- Using a sheet of chart paper for each, identify several different cultural groups. Have student cut pictures from magazines that reflect specific individual cultures. Discuss stereotyping, taking care to avoid including items that are typically thought of as stereotypic of a particular group.

## Recommended Children's Books

Friedman, I. (1987). *How My Parents Learned to Eat*. Houghton Mifflin.
Hollyer, B. (1999). *Wake Up, World: A Day in the Life of Children around the World*. H. Holt and Company.
Kindersley, B. (1995). *Children Just Like Me*. Dorling Kindersley.
Krupinski, L. (1998). *Best Friends*. Hyperion.
Roundtree, K. (1996). *A Carp for Kimiko*. Charlesbridge Publishing.
Also see Recommended Children's Books, chapter 9.

## Technology Resources

www.cherokee.org/Culture/Kids.asp: Games, stories, and facts for students about Cherokee culture.

www.geocities.com/resats/culture.html: Turkish culture site with music, folk dances, art, games, folk knowledge, and a variety of other information and activities.

www.armory.com/~web.jbooks.html: An annotated bibliography of children's books about Jewish religion and culture.

## DIVERSITY DURING WESTWARD EXPANSION

Students will explore the reasons for immigration by diverse groups to the western territories.

Duration: several class periods
Group Size: pairs
Disciplines: history, geography, language arts, fine arts
Skills: describing, interpreting, deducing, generalizing, analyzing, inferring
Key Vocabulary: transcontinental railroad, immigration, emigration, laborer, west, immigrant, unskilled, homeland, discrimination, diversity
Materials: drawing paper, markers or crayons, world map

**Procedure**

1. Read and discuss the information found in appendix C. Adjust terminology to be most appropriate for given grade levels.
2. Identify North America's western territories and origins of diverse populations on the map and mark for future reference.
3. Have students provide an oral retelling of the information. As they provide information, model sentence writing by placing the individual facts on drawing paper. Review by having students organize the information sequentially.
4. Divide students into small groups. Provide each group (or student) with one of the fact pages constructed in the previous step. Have them illustrate the information found on their page. When completed, hang the fact pages in the room. Discuss various groups that traveled west, focusing on the origins from which many of these European settlers and their ancestors came (Irish, Scottish, etc.)

## Extensions/Adaptations

- Construct a retelling of *The Iron Dragon Never Sleeps* using the writing, model, and illustration method.
- Locate illustrations on websites related to the Chinese and westward expansion. Print these out and attach them in collage form to information pages.
- Construct murals on newsprint to represent the story of the (Chinese, Jewish, etc.) emigration and immigration.
- Set up a center area for work on illustrations. Students can work on their information page with teacher input and direction as needed.

## Recommended Children's Books

Hoobler, Dorothy. (1999). *Chinese American Family Album*. Econoclad Books.

Katz, William Loren. (1995). *Black Women of the Old West*. Simon and Schuster.

Katz, William Loren. (1996). *The Black West: A Documentary and Pictorial History of the African American Role in the Westward Expansion of the U.S.* Simon and Schuster.

Krensky, Stephen. (1995). *The Iron Dragon Never Sleeps*. Bantam Doubleday Books.

Sandler, Martin W. (1994). *Pioneers*. Harper Collins Juvenile Books.

Sonneborn, L. (2002). *American West: An Illustrated History*. Scholastic.

Yee, Paul. (1999). *Tales from the Gold Mountain: Stories of the Chinese in the New World*. Groundwork Books.

## Technology Resources

dizzy.library.arizona.edu/images/chamer/railroad_041801.html: A historical perspective on the early Chinese immigrants brought to Arizona on the Southern Pacific Railroad to work in the mines and on extending the railroad through the desert.

www.newton.mec.edu/Angier/DimSum/Emigration%Reading%20Lessons .htm: "The Gold Rush: An Immigrant's Perspective" provides information about Chinese, American Indians, African Americans, and Latinos during the western expansion and provides their perspectives using primary visual sources and historical documents.

xroads.virginia.edu/~MAP/terr_hp.html: Viewer clicks on a date and can view any U.S. territorial maps from 1775 to 1920.

## ALL KINDS OF HOMES

Students will compare and contrast various home types and the diverse people with whom these homes are associated.

Duration: 1–2 class periods
Group Size: individuals
Disciplines: history, geography, language arts, fine arts
Skills: describing, interpreting, deducing, generalizing, analyzing, inferring
Key Vocabulary: identify names for house located in *This Is My House*
Materials: drawing paper, markers or crayons, yarn or string, local map, U.S. and world maps

### Procedure

1. Read the book *This Is My House* together. Discuss, focusing primarily on the different types of people and homes illustrated in the book. Show on maps where these homes and people are located.
2. Send home a letter of request to parents and have students bring a photo of their home to class. Glue each home picture to a large sheet of construction paper.
3. Students will draw pictures of their family members. Students then label family members and provide a written description of their houses.
4. Post pictures on a local map, using yarn or string to connect the pictures with actual locations on the map.
5. Discuss similarities and differences among families and places where families live. Generate a web that identifies what all families have in common, most families have in common, and some families have in common.

### Extensions/Adaptations

- Make copies of homes and people from the book. Have students match these with locations on U.S. and world maps and link them with yarn or string.

- Compare and contrast homes and people from around the world (as identified in *People*) with those generated by the students.
- For a final project, have the students form groups and research a type of house. Have them build a model. Display the finished products.

## Recommended Children's Books

Angelou, Maya. (2003). *My Painted House, My Friendly Chicken, and Me*. Crown Books for Young Readers.

Cameron, Ann. (1993). *The Most Beautiful Place in the World*. Yearling Books.

Dorros, A. (1992). *This is My House*. Scholastic.

Garza, Carmen Lomas. (1990). *Cuadros de familia/Family Pictures*. CBA.

Herrara, Juan Felipe. (2001). *Calling the Doves/El Canto De Las Palomas*. Children's Book Press.

Komatsu, Yoshio. (2004). *Wonderful Houses Around the World*. Shelter Publications, Incorporated.

Morris, Ann. (1995). *Houses and Homes*. William Morrow and Company.

Spier, Peter. (1988). *People*. Doubleday Publishing.

## Technology Resources

www.germantown.k12.il.us/indians/southwest.html: A look at the homes and culture of the Anasazi, Pueblo, and Hopi tribes.

asiarecipe.com/chidaiculture.html: Pictures and discussion of the Dai (southwest China) culture and bamboo houses.

www.humnet.ucla.edu/aflang/zulu/culture.html: Photos and text describing a number of facets of the Zulu culture of Africa.

## PEOPLE OF THE WEST

Students will become familiar with specific previously unknown people representing several cultures involved in settling the western territories.

Duration: 3–4 class periods

Group Size: 2–3

Disciplines: history, geography, sociology, language arts

Skills: describing, generalizing, interpreting, analyzing, record keeping
Key Vocabulary: contributions, territorial, cultural, expedition, affiliation
Materials: writing and drawing materials, Internet and library access, 4 × 6 index cards

## Procedure

1. Review information about cultural groups traveling to the West.
2. Allow student groups to select one of the following people (or groups) on which to report (others can be added to the list):

| | | |
|---|---|---|
| York (part of the Lewis and Clark expedition) | Chief Joseph | Bose Ikard |
| | Charley Lee Groceries | The Spiegelberg family |
| | Abraham & Zadoc Staab | |
| Jim Beckwourth | Little Crow | Jim Fowler |
| Coolies | Jim Perry | Nathan Bibo |
| Ying On Association | Aaron & Louis Zeckendorf | One Horse Charley |
| George Bush (1800s) | Red Cloud | The Exodusters |

3. Research should focus on important contributions, associated dates, territorial affiliation, and cultural affiliation. Remind students to focus on the 1800s when locating information on the Internet.
4. Information from research should be summarized on one side of the index cards. Do not include the name of the person on the card. Illustrate some aspect of research on the back side of each index card. Put the name of the person on a separate index card. (Identify each pair of cards by a unique symbol placed discretely on the front of each card so they can be used in a variety of ways).
5. Students share clues with other class members and evaluate information to determine who each person is.

## Extensions/Adaptations

- Create a speech similar to one the researched person might have given to present information about the person.

- Have students develop card sets into various card games for reinforcement of information.

## Recommended Children's Books

Byars, Betsy. (1989). *The Golly Sisters Go West*. Harper Collins.
Carmack, Melanie Z. (1997). *P is for Pioneer*. Buffalo Books.
Cordier, Mary Hurlbut. (1989). *Peoples of the American West: Historical Perspectives through Children's Literature*. Scarecrow Press Incorporated.
Fifer, B. (2000). *Going Along with Lewis and Clark*. Faircountry Press.
Sandler, Martin W. (1994). *Pioneers*. Harper Collins Juvenile Books.
Schnazer, R. (2002). *How We Crossed the West: The Adventures of Lewis and Clark*. National Geographic.
Swain, Gwenyth. (1999). *Civil Rights Pioneer*. Lerner Publishing Group.
See also biographies of individuals.

## Technology Resources

www.over-land.com/westpers2/html: "Women of the West" provides viewers with the opportunity to select a woman by name and view illustrations, photographs, and information about the person.
www.pbs.org/weta/thewest/people: "People in the West" includes information on famous pioneers who helped settle the West. The viewer clicks on the name of the person and links to information and illustrations.
www.surfnetkids.com/lewisclark.htm: A virtual Lewis and Clark expedition in which students can become involved.

## THE CHALLENGE OF BELONGING

Using prior knowledge, prediction, and problem solving to make decisions, students will engage in simulations focusing on the decision-making process and how this process continues to survive throughout history and in various cultures.

Duration: varies
Group Size: individual, small group, and whole class
Disciplines: geography, philosophy, sociology, language arts, science

Skills: communicating, problem solving, analyzing, decision making, inferring, hypothesizing, predicting
Key Vocabulary: immigrants, immigrations, ethnicity, cultural diversity
Materials: *The Green Book*, writing materials, voyage list handout/overhead, Acadian Journey description

## Procedure

*Part 1*

1. Discuss with students the necessity for planning ahead when taking a trip. Ask questions such as the following: What types of things might you take when you go on a short trip? What types of things might you take when you go on a trip and will be gone for a week? When we go for trips today, do we need to take things such as food, medicine kits, blankets, and so on? Why or why not? When would a person need to pack things such as blankets, books, and the like when going on a trip? When going on the kind of trip that would necessitate taking blankets, books, and so on, what other types of things might a person want to take? Why?
2. Show students a copy of the voyage list, which follows, on the overhead projector.

| | | |
|---|---|---|
| saw, ax, and hammer | camera | medicine kit |
| book | seeds (vegetable | fishing pole |
| photographs | and grain) | and tackle |
| family pet | seeds (flowers) | clothing (warm |
| shovel | gun and bullets | weather) |
| pots and pans | sewing machine | hunting knife |
| matches or lighter | (with thread) | clothing (cold weather) |
| blankets | dishes | candles and matches |

3. Provide students with the following directions:

   a. Pretend you are moving to a new home about which you know nothing.
   b. There is not a lot of room in the vehicle in which you will be traveling, so you have been told you can only take the eight items you feel are most important to have.

   c. Make a list of the eight items you (individually) would want to take.

   d. Number the items on your list, with 1 being most important, 2 being next, and so on.

4. Discuss individual choices as a group, being sure that all selections are reinforced as being correct since these are individual choices with no right or wrong answers.

5. Briefly summarize *The Green Book* by reading pages 3 through 7. Identify one of the purposes for reading the book: to determine if their choices about what to take on their imaginary move to a new home would be different given a specific set of circumstances.

## Part 2

Read the book with the students over a several-day period. Review and discuss story components from pages 8, 13, 34–35, 63, and 68–69 upon completion of the book. (This is important to the decision-making process).

## Part 3

1. Provide the voyage list once again on the overhead. Have students examine their original lists. Allow students to revise their lists given a new set of circumstances: they will be traveling in a spacecraft to make their new home on Shine.

2. Discuss revisions and reasons for revisions. Stress that certain selections are more appropriate for this particular journey and why (e.g., Earth seeds would not grow on Shine because of the alien soil).

3. Discuss how history is full of people from many different cultures and countries who have had to move from one home to another.

4. Generate a list of examples such as the following: Pilgrims coming from England to the New World, Irish immigrating to the United States from Ireland, Westward expansion in North America, Acadians from Nova Scotia to South Louisiana, Amish/Mennonite populations from various countries in Europe to the United States.

## Extensions/Adaptations

- Historical topics can change depending on suitability for grade level.
- Conduct the entire activity in a large group setting. Decisions are based on group majority (or group consensus, if possible).
- Allow groups to be of different sizes to replicate more accurately how different-sized family groups would have differing priorities.
- Plan a picnic to a park. List all possible items to be taken. Limit the number of items that can be selected.

## Recommended Children's Books

Berger, M. (1993). *Where Did Your Family Come From?* Hambleton-Hill Publishing Company.

Figueredo, D. (1999). *When the World Was New.* Lee and Low Books.

Hesse, K. (1993). *Letters from Rifkin.* Penguin Putnam Books.

Knight, M. (1993). *Who Belongs Here? An American Story.* Tilbury House Publishers.

Sandler, M. (2000). *Immigrants.* Harper Collins.

Walsh, J. (1982). *The Green Book.* New York: Farrar, Straus, and Giroux.

## Technology Resources

www.acadian-cajun.com: Acadian and Cajun history and genealogy site, time lines, and links.

www.coloradocollege.edu/Dept/HY243Ruiz/Research/diaspora.html: A brief history of the African Diaspora.

www.yvwiiusdinvnohii.net/articles/princes.html: Accounts of the Cherokee Trail of Tears.

# CHAPTER 2

# Time, Continuity, and Change

A people without history is like wind upon the buffalo grass.

—Teton Sioux Indians

However far the stream flows, it never forgets its source.

—West African Yoruba

In simple terms, history is time, continuity, and change—the study of the past, what happened and why it happened. From before the time of the Greeks and Romans, storytellers, bards, and priests used the oral tradition of storytelling to pass along information to succeeding generations. History enables us to understand our place in the stream of time and to make some sense of the story of our lives and the lives of our ancestors. Perhaps more poetically, history is remembrance, the key to who we once were and from whence we came. Traditionally, the teaching of history has been left primarily to factual content presented within conventional textbooks. However, because the study of history is personal, an effective study of history must involve more than the passive absorption and regurgitation of information about people, places, and dates.

When addressing time, continuity, and change in grades K–4, the focus must address not only facts but, more importantly, thinking skills related to historical chronology, comprehension, analysis and interpretation, and analysis and decision making. The skills, while identified separately, are not mutually exclusive but should complement one another. Activities that focus on history and sociology can effectively speak to topics that address social perspectives throughout history and comparisons of the past and its relationship to our present-day global society. The study of time, continuity, and change will allow students to use their knowledge of the past to make informed decisions in the present and about the future.

## WAGONS WESTWARD HO!

Students will draw a representation of a Conestoga wagon to full scale and will reconstruct a physical representation of the Conestoga wagon used as a mode of travel by some pioneers who traveled west.

Duration: 5–6 class periods
Group Size: 4–5
Disciplines: history, math, fine arts, language arts
Skills: describing, interpreting, deducing, experimenting, generalizing, analyzing, inferring
Key Vocabulary: wagon trains, provisions, Great Plains, Great American Desert, pioneers, territories, transcontinental railroad, Conestoga wagon, feed box, lazy board, barrel, length, height, width, cover, tongue, wood bows, replica, sturdy
Materials: Part 1: sidewalk chalk, Conestoga wagon information and picture, meter sticks or yard sticks; Part 2: per group: rubber cement, craft sticks, cloth, construction paper, string, rulers, writing materials, picture of Conestoga wagon

### Procedure

*Part 1*

1. Read the story about Grandma Essie, *Grandma Essie's Covered Wagon*, and discuss the story through questions such as, Why did the family decide to go west? How did the family take care of themselves on the journey? What was the home like in the western part of Kansas? Why did they have to leave Kansas? Why did Grandma Essie's family crate the strawberries and ship them by train?
2. Using the website www.museumeducation.org/curricula_phototour_camino09.html, summarize information that describes

the Spanish settlers, including children on horseback and in carretas, who traveled into the Southwest (New Spain).

3. Tell students they are going to pretend they are part of a family,
similar to one of those in the stories, traveling to the West in
search of a better life. They are only able to carry a certain
amount of supplies on their wagon because of the size.

4. Place a picture of the Conestoga wagon on the overhead and discuss its physical characteristics. Appropriate diagrams are located
at www.oregontrail.blm.gov/wagons.htm and www.rootsweb.com/
~pacahs/wagon.htm.

5. Take the class outside to a designated area (playground, parking
lot, etc.). Using the information and measuring devices, draw an
outline of the Conestoga wagon in the correct dimensions. Line
students up along the outline to show length, then width, then
height. Compare the size of the Conestoga wagon to current-day
items for students to understand the concept of the wagon's size.

6. Once inside again, place the picture of the Conestoga wagon back
on the overhead projector and discuss the components.

## Part 2

1. Compare the Conestoga wagon with the Spanish carreta. Using
natural materials and a picture of the Spanish carreta, have the
students work cooperatively to construct a wagon scene including
a miniature of the carreta.

2. Since the wagon was "up to" 11 feet by 24 feet, discuss that some
wagons would be a little smaller and some a little larger than the
one we have marked out. Identify the specific size of the wagon
to be replicated: $24 \times 12 \times 6$. For this activity, 1/2 inch = 1 foot.
(e.g., the length of a 24-foot wagon = $24 \times 1/24 = 24/24 = 1$
foot. This is the equivalent of two craft sticks when each craft
stick is 6 inches long. Therefore, the length of the model wagon,
based on a real wagon that is 24 feet long, would be 1 foot long.)
For younger children, you may want to increase the size to make
working conditions easier.

3. Discuss aspects of building the wagon such as, What types of jobs
did you do as you constructed the wagon? What types of jobs might

have been needed when constructing a real carreta? What was the hardest part about building the wagon? What was the easiest part? Why did the pioneers need to be sure that their wagons were well built? What would happen if their wagons were not sturdy?

## Extensions/Adaptations

- Place several students in the position of the draught animals at the front of the wagon so that students can see how long the wagon would be including the animals.
- Outline the wagon on the playground (using flour) prior to taking students outside.
- Identify groups and jobs for each person in each group, for example, gluer, board placer, board holder, fabric sewer, and so on.
- Using an enlargement of a Conestoga wagon picture, have students glue craft sticks, cloth, and other materials onto the appropriate places.
- In the 1850s, U.S. attorney for the New Mexico territory, William Watts Hart Davis, said this about the carreta: "The wheels are never greased, and as they are driven along they make an unearthly sound." What would be an advantage and a disadvantage of this aspect of the carreta? Why?
- Discuss: Drivers of the carreta were afraid that if the wheels of the wagon were oiled, evil spirits would interfere with the trip, whereas the screeching sounds scared the evil spirits away.
- More than one wagon scene could be constructed using different dimensions and scenery for each.
- Consider this an ongoing activity that students can work on at various times during the day for several days of the unit.

## Recommended Children's Books

Erikson, Paul. (1997). *Daily Life in a Conestoga Wagon*. Puffin Books.
Levin, Ellen. (1992). *If You Traveled in a Covered Wagon*. Scholastic.
Patent, Dorothy Henshaw. (1995). *Travels by Wagon*. Walker and Company.
Richard, Ammon. (2000). *Conestoga Wagons*. Holiday House.
Williams, David. (1993). *Grandma Essie's Covered Wagon*. Alfred A. Knopf Publishing.

## Technology Resources

www.museumeducation.org/curricula_phototour_camino09.html: Provides information on and pictures of horsedrawn carros and carretas in the Southwest.

www.pbs.org/wnet/frontierhouse/frontierlife/essay2.html: Stories and photographs provide information about packing the Conestoga wagon and heading west, including actual supply and weight lists.

www.ourworld.compuserve.com/homepages/trailofthe49ers/wagons.htm: Diagrams and descriptions of three types of covered wagons are provided.

www.sover.net/~barback/ot/wagons.html: "Wagons on the Trail West" provides illustrations, information, and photographs of travel west in various covered wagons but focuses primarily on the Conestoga.

## BREAKFAST WITH WASHINGTON

Students will prepare breakfast foods and will compare breakfast foods from the time of George Washington with breakfast foods of today.

Duration: 1–3 class sessions

Group Size: whole class and groups of 3–5

Skills: hypothesizing, communicating, analyzing, comparing/contrasting

Disciplines: sociology, language arts, math, health, history

Key Vocabulary: hoecakes, "in Washington's day," usual, namesake, Father of our Country

Materials: pictures of various breakfast foods (modern breakfast foods: boxed cereal, bacon, English muffins, biscuits, toaster strudels, etc.; historical breakfast foods: porridge, johnnycake, hasty pudding, etc.), food and recipe magazines, large mixing bowl, water, spoon, flour, measuring cup, electric griddle, garden hoe, paper plates

### Procedure

*Part 1*

1. Brainstorm items that the students usually eat for breakfast. Brainstorm items that they think George Washington might have eaten for breakfast (on a separate list).

2. Read *George Washington's Breakfast* and keep a list of the different types of food about which George Washington Allen finds information.
3. Draw a chart with two columns: Breakfast Foods Today and Breakfast Foods in Washington's Day.
4. Allow students to (1) select pictures that illustrate the types of food in the book, (2) select modern-day foods with which to compare, and (3) attach pictures of the foods to the chart.
5. Discuss tastes of the various foods.

*Part 2*

1. Prepare several types of foods identified on the charts and in the book (e.g., pancakes, hoecakes, johnnycakes, cereal, hasty pudding, porridge). For each food prepared, discuss the ingredients and how the food was (or is) actually prepared.
2. Compare present-day food taste and cooking methods with foods of the past such as hoecakes vs. pancakes, cereal vs. hasty pudding, oatmeal vs. porridge.
3. Discuss the similarities and differences in tastes, ingredients, cooking methods, availability of ingredients, and amount of time needed to cook various items. Discuss how the foods Washington ate at home might compare with foods he ate while on the march or camped with the army.

**Extensions/Adaptations**

- Divide the class into groups and allow groups to measure and mix ingredients for various foods.
- Older students can pour the ingredients onto the griddle or skillet themselves.
- With the permission of school administration, cook traditional hoecakes outside over a fire.
- Set up the room in learning centers with each center focusing on a particular food type. Students measure and cook enough food for the entire class within the individual centers and then share the food with the rest of the class.

- Focus on the research process through which George Washington Allen (GWA) proceeds as he looks for answers to his questions. Identify other questions about George Washington that GWA might have. Work in groups to research these questions in the library and through other sources.
- Provide food magazines. Allows students to cut and paste pictures of traditional and modern foods onto charts categorized by type.
- Using pictures from food magazines, have students cut out pictures of traditional and modern foods and categorize them according to the food pyramid. Discuss the health benefits.
- Focus on phrases, slogans, and quotes from Washington's day: Father of Our Country, The Swamp Fox, "Give me liberty or give me death," and the like. Discuss the influence of ideas related to these items.
- Discuss aspects of Washington such as his military and political leadership during the Revolutionary War.
- Incorporate favorite snack foods as part of the lesson: 1860 chewing gum, 1877 root beer, 1890 hot dog, 1912 Oreos, 1945 pizza, 1968 Big Mac, and so on. Discuss healthy vs. nonhealthy foods. Select which might have been George Washington's favorites or what foods discussed earlier might have been favorites and why.

## Recommended Children's Books

Brooks, F., Bond, S., & Evans, C. (eds.). (1989). *Find Out about Food and Eating Long Ago*. ECDP.

Erdosh, G. (dates vary). *Cooking throughout American History Series*. Rosen Publishing Group.

Fritz, Jean. (1998). *George Washington's Breakfast*. Putnman & Grosset Publishing Group.

Harness, C. (1999). *George Washington*. National Geographic Society.

Ichord, L. (1999). *Hasty Pudding, Johnnycake, and other Good Stuff: Cooking in Colonial America*. Millbrook Press.

Ventura, Piero. (1994). *Food: Its Evolution through the Ages*. Houghton Mifflin.

Woods, A. (1992). *Young George Washington: America's First President*. Troll Communications.

**Technology Resources**

odur.let.rug.nl/~usa/P/gw1/gw1.htm: Speeches, papers, and messages of George Washington.

www.mountvernon.org/learn/meet_george/index.cfm/: Biography lesson about George Washington with interactive activities for students and resources for teachers.

www.osv.org/gw/wquiz2.htm: Interactive information regarding myths and truths about George Washington.

## LEARNING FROM THE CEMETERY

Use of the local cemetery enables students to collect, categorize, analyze, and present data in 3-D time-line form as well as to learn about people, places, and events that are part of a community's history. "Reading" monuments can provide information related to the age of the community, its ethnic composition, and possible impacts made by immigration as well as reflect religious beliefs, social class and values, and cultural change over time.

Duration: field trip plus approximately 4–5 fifty-minute class periods

Group Size: individually or pairs at the cemetery; whole class upon return

Skills: classifying, analyzing, communicating, collaborating, measuring, inferring

Disciplines: history, ecology, language arts, mathematics, science, anthropology, fine arts

Key Vocabulary: select appropriate vocabulary from glossary of symbols and glossary of terms at the end of this activity

Materials: writing materials, drawing/coloring materials

**Procedure**

*Part 1: Prior to Arriving at the Cemetery*

Discuss: (a) vocabulary appropriate for grade level from glossaries of symbols and terms, (b) the cemetery as a big jigsaw puzzle rather than as a scary place (the puzzle holds clues to the history of the community and the people who once lived there), (c) the type of data students might expect to find on a gravestone, and (d) basic cemetery etiquette, as follows:

- Treat all graves with respect.
- Leave all artifacts and flowers as you find them.
- Keep voices low in respect for others who may be visiting the cemetery.
- Leave no litter. Pick up any trash and put it in the appropriate place.
- Remember, the cemetery is not a playground.

*Part 2: On Location*

Assign various students to research certain parts of the cemetery to avoid as much data-card redundancy as possible. Have students work individually or in teams of two to collect data on cemetery data cards. On index cards, students should include the following:

- name
- birth date
- date of death
- age at death
- male or female

*Part 3: Upon Return to the Classroom*

1. Orally review the names located on the data cards and eliminate those that are redundant.
2. Place newsprint, butcher paper, or perforated computer paper on the floor in a large area.
3. Identify with the students the oldest and newest dates located in the cemetery. Use these dates to assist students in drawing a time line, with increments of ten years, on the paper. Have students place cards one above the other according to one selected specific criteria: age at death, date of birth, date of death. Separate criteria cards for each time period into two columns according to gender.

4. Dependent upon card distribution for each selected criteria, research and discuss the following items: What generalizations can you make about the distribution of the information on the time line? What events in history can be logically connected with the large number of deaths in a specific decade? What local events can be attributed to the large number of deaths in a specific decade? In any given year, which group of people, adults or children, male or female, are represented by the greatest number? What incidents might contribute to this representation of one group over the other? In a specific decade, why were so many tombstones for people under the age of (select an age)? What global events might be attributed to birth and death rates during specific time periods?

## Extensions/Adaptations

* Demonstrate rubbing technique and have individuals take rubbings from various gravestones. Imagery can be discussed upon returning to the classroom.
* Encourage students to write a cinquain or diamante about their feelings as they sit quietly under a tree or somewhere peaceful. Discuss cemeteries as being peaceful rather than scary.
* Encourage mapping skills by having students construct a visual representation of parts of the cemetery, including a rose compass, scale, boundaries, and the like.
* Add components to data cards: copy inscription/epitaph exactly as it occurs; sketch the shape of the gravestone; identify any motifs on the gravestone such as military affiliations, honors, and so on; identify any related person buried near the gravestone and identify their relationship to the person.

## Recommended Children's Books

Ross, K., & Ross, A. (1995). *Cemetery Quilt*. Houghton Mifflin.
Shafer, J. (1988). *Right in Your Own Backyard: A Unit of Study for Local History*. River Road Publishing.
Stein, R. (1996). *Arlington National Cemetery*. Children's Press.
Weitzman, D. (1975). *My Backyard History Book*. Little, Brown and Company.

## Technology Resources

www.daddezio.com/cemetery/index.html: Directions for cemeteries and links
  to interesting websites.
www.cemetery.state.tx.us: A memorial site for honored deceased Texans.
www.arlingtoncemetery.com/: Site dedicated to national heroes at the Arlington National Cemetery.

## Glossary of Symbols

| Symbols | Interpretations |
| --- | --- |
| angel, flying | rebirth, joy |
| angel weeping or weeping willow | grief, sorrow |
| arch, garland, or wreath | victory of life or victory in death |
| bird | eternal life |
| bird in flight or winged skull | flight of the soul |
| candle, flame, tree, or tree sprouting; sun shining or rising | life, renewed life |
| columns or doors | heavenly entrance |
| dove | purity, devotion |
| figs or pineapples | prosperity, friendship |
| flower | frailty of life |
| heart | love |
| hourglass | time's passing |
| lamb | innocence |
| pall, pick, severed branch, spade, skull, or skeleton | mortality |
| scythe, sun setting, or wheat sheaves | death |
| thistle | of Scottish descent |

## Glossary of Terms

| Terms | Definitions |
| --- | --- |
| AE | abbreviation for Aetatis, years of life |
| B.P.O.E. | Benevolent Protective Order of Elks |
| cemetery | a place for burying the dead |
| consort | a husband alive at the time of his wife's death |

| C.S.A. | Confederate States Army |
| D.S.P (Latin) or obit sine prole | died without children |
| D.V.P. (Latin) | died in father's lifetime |
| D.Y. | died young |
| epitaph | an inscription on a tombstone or monument in memory of the person buried |
| foot stone | a stone marking the foot of a grave |
| G.A.R. | Grand Army of the Republic |
| gravestone | a stone that marks a grave |
| headstone | a memorial stone set at the head of a grave |
| H.S. (Latin) | here is buried |
| I.H.S. | Greek spelling of Christ |
| I.O.O.F. | Independent Order of Odd Fellows |
| obit | died |
| O.E.S. | Order of Eastern Star |
| relict | a widow |
| sarcophagus | an ornamental stone coffin |
| V.F.W. | Veteran of Foreign Wars |

## THE DILEMMA

Students determine benefits and consequences of decisions made related to events of World War II.

Duration: 1 class session
Group Size: small groups of 3–4
Skills: inferring, predicting, decision making
Disciplines: history, sociology, philosophy, language arts
Key Vocabulary: deport, Nazi, Jewish, concentration camps, Gestapo, World War II
Materials: dilemma information, decision-making table

### Procedure

*Part 1*

1. Divide class into student groups of four to five. Read dilemma information aloud to students and place a copy of the information

on the overhead so students can reread as needed. Provide adequate time for students to discuss the issue and to decide upon a course of action. Consensus should be reached if possible.

*Dilemma Information.* From the time they were babies, Rachel and Anna had grown up together. They were best friends even though Anna's family was Christian and Rachel's family was Jewish. For many years this religious difference didn't matter in Germany, but after Hitler became the country's leader, the situation changed. Hitler required Jewish people to wear armbands or badges with a yellow Star of David on them. He began to encourage his followers to destroy the property of the Jewish people and to beat them on the streets. Finally, he began to have Jewish families arrested and deported. Rumors began that the families being deported were killed. Because of the rumors, many people tried to offer hiding places for Jewish families. Hitler organized a secret police, the Gestapo, one of whose jobs was to look for Jewish families in hiding. If the Gestapo located a family and those who had helped hide the family, it was considered a serious crime, one that violated the laws of the German government.

One night Anna heard a knock at the door of her family's home. When she opened the door, she found Rachel on the step huddled in a dark coat. Quickly Rachel stepped inside the door and closed it behind her. She had been to a meeting, she said, and when she returned home, she had found Gestapo members all around her house. Her parents, brothers, and sister had already been taken away. The houses next to her own had been dark, with no lights shining in any windows. Knowing her fate if the Gestapo found her, Rachel had run to Anna's home a few blocks away.

Anna was stunned. If she turned Rachel away, the Gestapo would eventually find her. Anna knew that most of the Jewish people who were said to have been deported had actually been killed, and she didn't want her best friend to die. But hiding anyone Jewish broke the law. If she hid Rachel, Anna was risking her own safety and that of her family. But she had a tiny room behind the chimney of the third floor where Rachel might be safe. Question: Should Anna hide Rachel? Why or why not?

2. Reconvene as a whole group and discuss the decisions of the groups. Discuss: Were enough facts presented for you to make a "good"

decision? If not, why not? What other facts were needed? What process did the group go through as they made their decisions?

*Part 2*

1. Discuss steps/process involved in decision making. Examine the decision-making table components located at the end of this lesson. Review the dilemma information. Construct and complete a two-column table as a class using the information gathered in the groups. Column one should consist of the decision-making components. Column two should consist of information generated by the students.
2. Begin reading *Number the Stars*. Provide time for students to convene in different groups for each decision that Annemarie has to make regarding her involvement with saving the Jewish population throughout the book. Have each group keep a "decision-making table" on each decision.
3. Categorize the decision-making tables once the reading has been completed. (Refer to the next section, "Decision-Making Table Information.") Discuss the following: changes in types of decisions made throughout the reading, reasons for changes in decision making, process involved in decision making, how these decision-making topics can (do) relate to decision making in real life, circumstances in which you may not go through a process when making a decision.
4. If consensus is impossible, allow the students to vote in small groups.

**Decision-Making Table Information**

First, all responses to moral dilemmas should be accepted. The teacher should not provide his or her response so as to avoid influencing student decisions. Second, the reasoning will reflect one of five aspects (or a combination of two), depending on the developmental level of individuals:

1. If Anna hides Rachel, she might also get in trouble with the Gestapo.

2. If the situation were reversed, Rachel probably wouldn't hide Anna, so in this case Anna shouldn't take a chance by hiding Rachel.
3. Anna's first concern (and obligation) is to her family. Therefore, she should not endanger them by hiding Rachel.
4. The laws of the government are in place for a reason. Anna should obey the laws if she expects other people to obey them as well.
5. Friendship and family are not the real issues. Anna should be helping all Jewish people if she is truly concerned about the problem in her society. She should not hide Rachel unless she intends to hide others and publicly protest the Jewish people's being deported and/or killed.

## Extensions/Adaptations

- Use dilemma in conjunction with the story of *Rose Blanche* for a simpler and less intense choice. (Should Rose have taken food to the little boy at the concentration camp?)
- Enlarge group size if students have had previous experience working with moral-dilemma decision making.
- Provide daily life examples with which to work for those students who have not worked with moral-dilemma decision making. Following are some examples:
  - You saw who stole your friend's bicycle, but the person who stole it is also your friend. What should you do?
  - Someone lost a wallet on the street, and you found it. It had one check for $100, $25 in cash, and a credit card plus identification. What will you do with the wallet and its contents?
  - Someone lost a wallet on the street, and you found it. It had one check for $100, $25 in cash, and a credit card but no owner identification. What will you do with the wallet and its contents?

## Recommended Children's Books

Emert, P. (1996). *True Valor: Stories of Brave Men and Women in World War II*. Lowell House Juvenile Books.
Greenfield, H. (1993). *The Hidden Children*. Ticknor and Fields.
Innocenti, R. (1999). *Rose Blanche*. EconoClad Books.

Lowry, Lois. (1990). *Number the Stars*. Bantam Doubleday Dell Books.

Sim, D. (1997). *In My Pocket*. Harcourt Brace and Company.

## Technology Resources

library.thinkquest.org/12663: A stark examination of the holocaust with many informative links.

www.lib.duke.edu/reference/holocast.htm: A site featuring book and article lists and links to related holocaust sites.

www.annefrank.com: The Anne Frank exhibit including student activities.

## Decision-Making Table Components

1. Topic/Issue/Event: Phrase the item in neutral terms (Hiding Rachel) or as a question (Should Anna hide Rachel?).
2. Identify important ideas found in the information that informed you about the issue.
3. Identify two options related to the topic: option A (hide Rachel) and option B (do not hide Rachel).
4. Identify four or five reasons for option A and option B. Reasons for each option are generated through a brainstorming session by the students. All answers are acceptable as long as they address the option.
5. Number each reason for option A according to its importance. Then number each reason for option B according to its importance. Students decide which reasons are important to them personally. They do not need to justify their reasoning.
6. Can a compromise between the two options be reached? Indicate Yes or No.
7. If a compromise can be reached, identify the compromise and provide reasons about why it seems to be a valid one. Students provide support of their compromise decision based on reasons.
8. If a compromise cannot be reached, review reasons for options A and B. Make a decision. Students select a decision: to hide Rachel or not to hide Rachel.
9. Identify the reasons (top 3) on which the decision was made.

## COWBOYS

The history of the American cowboy is reflected in the clothing and equipment used by cowboys today.

Duration: 1 class period
Group Size: individuals or pairs
Skills: observing, classifying, analyzing, communicating, collaborating
Disciplines: history, geography, language arts, fine arts, science
Key Vocabulary: vaqueros, mixed-bag, bandana, rolled slicker, saddle-horn lariat, longhorns
Materials: duplicated cowboy and equipment information, writing materials

**Procedure**

1. Discuss the information about the American cowboys (see appendix C).
2. Provide each student with the diagram located under the heading "Relate Images to Cowboys" at www.historyonthenet.com/Lessons/worksheets/american_west.htm. Have students describe how each image is related to the American cowboy and identify two ways in which each item could be used.
3. Enlarge the picture of the cowboy and equipment, located at the above website under the heading "Cowboy Picture," onto a transparency and copy the transparency onto chart paper. Provide students with opportunities to fill in the information onto the chart paper. Display in the classroom.
4. Discuss information about the camel cowboys of the Australian outback (www.abc.net.au/landline/archives/LandlineSubjectIndx_People.htm) and the Brazilian Pantaneiro cowboy (www.lagamar.com/Pages/p_man.html).
5. Compare and contrast the various responsibilities, physical characteristics, attitudes, and equipment of these two types of cowboys with the American cowboy. Discuss how geographic location affects these points of discussion.

## Extensions/Adaptations

- Compare the lives of cowboys today with those of the first cowboys, the Vaqueroes. (www.tpwd.state.tx.us/park/jose/vaquero.htm)
- Using the section entitled "Life of a Cowboy" from the above website, match the pictures and the statements provided and discuss the daily life of the cowboy.
- Locate additional websites that address cowboys from other areas of the world. How are these similar and different from those already discussed?
- Provide drawing paper and allow students to construct a scene from the late 1800s (in any location) that includes a cowboy and equipment that is specific to that area (such as the following). Label all items and develop an open-ended scenario to accompany the illustration.

1. Wide-brimmed hat
2. Boots with tall heels, high insteps, and pointed toes
3. Flap pockets
4. Rolled slicker

5. Leather chaps
6. Bandanna
7. Saddle horn
8. Gloves with cuffs

## Recommended Children's Books

Brimner, Larry D. (1999). *Cowboy Up!* Children's Press.
Freedman, Russell. (1990). *Cowboys of the Wild West*. Clarion Books.
Gagliano, Eugene. (2003). *C is for Cowboy*. Sleeping Bear Press.
Granfield, L. (1994). *Cowboy: An Album*. Tichnor and Fields.
Harrison, Peter. (2004). *Amazing World of the Wild West*. Anness Publishers Ltd.
Lowe, P., & Pike, J. (2000). *Desert Cowboy*. Megabala Books.
Myers, Walter Dean. (1999). *The Journal of Joshua Loper: A Black Cowboy*. Scholastic Books.
Teague, Mark. (1997). *How I Spent My Summer Vacation*. Dragonfly Books.
Tucker, Kathy. (1999). *Do Cowboys Ride Bikes?* Albert Whitman and Company.

## Technology Resources

www.nationalcowboymuseum.org/m_tour_el.html: Pictures and narrative present a variety of information related to the American cowboy.

www.focustours.com/panatanal.html: General information regarding the Pantanal area and cowboys with links to information on eco-tours.

www.geocities.com/Athens/Troy/9713: Information including photos and drawings of cowboy life that focuses on the history of the black cowboy.

studentweb.fontbonne.edu/~jhaar565/webquest: Cowboy Roundup provides information and activities to explore the lifestyle of the American cowboy.

# CHAPTER 3

# People, Places, and Environments

A civilization flourishes when people plant trees under whose shade they will never sit.

—Greek proverb

This Greek proverb is truly applicable when reflecting on the need for geographic studies, as it emphasizes the need for everyone to become aware of the interrelationships and interdependence among all people, locations, and systems found on the Earth's surface. Knowledge of geography, people, locations and habitats, and the relationships worldwide among the three directly impacts a person's ability to be an informed citizen able to address life's situations in various contexts. In doing this, individuals must have well-developed problem-solving, decision-making, and creative- and critical-thinking skills. Those who are not aware of geographic relationships outside their immediate environment will lack the knowledge needed to understand similarities and differences around the world.

Teaching geography through the use of media, including globes, maps, diagrams, charts, tables, and photographs, enables abstract concepts to be more easily understood. The teaching and learning of geographical concepts should include activities that use these materials to accomplish the following: provide students with exposure to many forms of geographic data, encourage encoding and decoding of material and information, offer opportunities to interpret changes around the world due to various events, connect past and present with predictions for the future, encourage appreciation of different aspects of the environment near and far, promote understanding of different peoples of the world based on their location, and link physical changes around the world to the impact of human distribution on earth.

## WHAT'S MY SHAPE?

Students will use shapes to identify locations within the United States and around the world.

Duration: 1 or more days
Group Size: individuals, small groups, large groups
Skills: describing, generalizing, classifying, evaluating
Disciplines: geography, fine arts, math
Key Vocabulary: appropriate state and regional names
Materials: maps of continents (2 each), overhead projector

### Procedure

1. Using one set of maps, cut out states, countries, and continents from maps and laminate.
2. Separate states into five areas: Northeast, Southeast, Northwest, Southwest, and Midwest. Divide countries according to continents.
3. Keep all pieces in separate, labeled ziplock bags.

*Part 1*

Have students match cutout countries, states, or continents with countries, states, or continents on full-sized maps.

*Part 2*

Place pieces from one ziplock bag on an overhead, one at a time, and then ask students to identify the state or country based on the shape.

### Extensions/Adaptations

- Eliminate names on the state or country pieces so students will match the pieces to the maps by using the shape only.

- Use a pocket chart and allow students to (a) match state shapes with state names; (b) match state shapes, names, and capital cities; (c) categorize shapes into regions; and (d) categorize shapes into similar shapes.
- Produce a large United States map on white paper and mount it on the classroom wall. Using magazines, have students locate pictures and words that describe various aspects of the state and glue in the appropriate location. Pictures and words cannot overlap state lines. This can also be done with individual countries or with continents.
- Place map pieces on historical maps (e.g., United States before all fifty states were established). Discuss changes from past to present. Predict possible future changes.
- Velcro can be placed on maps and individual map pieces. By placing maps and ziplock bags on a wall or bulletin board, students have the opportunity of working with an interactive bulletin board at various times during the day.

### Recommended Children's Books

Gordon, Patricia. (1999). *Kids Learn America*. Williamson Publishing.

Guthrie, Woody. (1998). *This Land Is Your Land*. Little, Brown and Company.

Hopkins, Lee Bennett. (2000). *My America: Poetry Atlas of the United States*. Simon and Schuster.

Keller, Laurie. (2002). *The Scrambled States of America*. Henry Holt and Company.

Krull, Kathleen. (1997). *Wish You Were Here: Emily's Guide to the 50 States*. Bantam Books.

Leedy, Loreen. (1999). *Celebrate the 50 States*. Holiday House.

*Ready To Go Super Book of Outline Maps*. (2000). Scholastic Books.

Rylant, Cynthia. (1998). *Tulip Sees America*. Scholastic Trade Books.

### Technology Resources

www.immigration-usa.com/maps/: An extensive collection of small countries around the world including maps to print and color.

www.goodeatlas.com/downloadmaps.htm: Access to printable maps of each state.

http://www.altapedia.com: Political maps of worldwide areas.

## LAND AND WATER MIX AND MATCH

Using definition cards, students will play a card game as they learn about various water and land forms.

Duration: 10–15 minutes
Group Size: full class, individually or in pairs
Skills: communication, classification
Disciplines: geography, ecology, language arts
Key Vocabulary: words related to water and land forms (copied onto index cards)
Materials: land and water cards (index cards)

### Procedure

Divide the class into groups of four or five. Provide each group with a set of cards. Content for cards is included at the end of this section. (For groups of four: each person gets five cards. For groups of five: each person gets four cards.)

*Part 1*

1. The group selects an "answer checker." This person places the answer key face down in the middle of the group.
2. One person in the group shuffles and deals the cards.
3. The person directly across from the dealer begins by selecting a card from the person to his or her right. If the card selected is the definition for a word card in his or her hand, the pair is placed faced up in front of the person.
4. The person reads the word card and definition aloud to the rest of the group.
5. If someone disagrees that the word is a match, the "answer checker" checks the answer key. If the cards are a match, play continues. If the cards do not match, the cards are returned to the original players and play continues with the next person drawing.
6. The person from whom the card was drawn then selects a card from the person to his or her right.

7. Play continues in this way until all pairs have been made.
8. If a player runs out of cards, he or she continues to draw (if possible) from the person on his or her right.
9. At the end of the game, the "answer checker" carefully checks the answers to make sure all pairs match.

*Part 2*

1. All cards are placed face down in the center of the group in rows.
2. Player 1 selects a card and then selects a second card, trying to find either the word or definition that goes with the first word.
3. As players locate pairs, the pairs are placed in front of the player obtaining the pair.
4. If a pair is not located, cards are replaced face down, and the person to Player 1's left turns over two cards.
5. Answers are checked against the answer key as they are found. If a pair is not a correct pair, the cards are replaced in the center of the group and play continues.
6. Play continues with each person getting one turn each time until all of the pairs have been matched.

*Part 3*

1. Separate the cards into word cards and definition cards. Half the students in a group get the word cards. The other half get the definition cards.
2. A player with a word card places any word card in the middle of the group face up.
3. A player with the appropriate definition card lays the card with the word card.
4. The person to the left of the person laying down the word card checks the answer.
5. Play continues with a definition card being placed down and a different person identifying the word card that goes with it.
6. Answer is checked. Play continues with word cards and definition cards being alternately put down first.

## Extensions/Adaptations

- Card games can be easily adapted to play with 1–4 players.
- Students can make up rules for new games or can use rules from other games about which they know. Divide the cards into separate sets (e.g., water forms and land forms; flat land and mountainous land).
- Sets of cards can be developed to accompany any content area topic in any discipline.

## Recommended Children's Books

American Education. (1999). *The Complete Book of Maps and Geography*. American Education Publishing Incorporated.

Guthrie, Woody. (1998). *This Land Is Your Land*. Little, Brown and Company.

Philip, George and Son. (1994). *Encyclopedic World Atlas: Country By Country Coverage*. Oxford University Press Incorporated.

Rand McNally Staff (1995). *GeoTrivia World*. Rand McNally Corporation.

TNT Stone Associates Staff. (1999). *Our Continents and Oceans*, Volume 17. Navigator Systems Incorporated.

## Technology Resources

earth.sea.int/rootcollection/eeo4.10075/ocean_page.html: A pictorial survey of oceanic phenomena visible to the naked eye from space.

www.ngdc.noaa.gov/mgg/image/: Images of world oceans and lakes from the World Data Center for Marine Geology and Geophysics.

www.gesource.ac.uk/worldguide/worldmap.html: Interactive world maps for students.

## Land and Water Card Information

| | |
|---|---|
| atoll | a ring-shaped coral island completely or nearly enclosing a body of water |
| basin | a region drained by a river and its tributaries |
| butte | a small steep-sided hill |
| canyon | a deep valley with very steep sides |
| coast | land beside a large body of water |

| | |
|---|---|
| delta | land formed by mud and sand that settled from water flowing out of the place where a river ends |
| desert | a region with very little rainfall and few plants |
| gulf | a part of an ocean or a sea that pushes inland |
| island | a body of land surrounded by water |
| lake | a body of fresh water (usually) surrounded by land |
| mountain | a section of land that rises sharply from the land that surrounds it |
| ocean | a very large body of salt water |
| peninsula | a strip of land with water on three sides, connected to a main body of land |
| plain | an almost level, often treeless piece of land that stretches for many miles |
| plateau | a raised, level section of land that covers a large area |
| prairie | an area of level or rolling grassland with few trees |
| sea | a body of salt water not as large as an ocean but larger than a lake |
| swamp | low, spongy land often covered with water |
| valley | a long, low place between hills or mountains that often has a stream or river |
| volcano | an opening in the earth, usually at the top of a cone-shaped hill, out of which steam and melted or hot rock may pour |

## THE RALLY

The simulation of a trip by car across various states will allow students to use scale and become familiar with locations of states as well as with cities within those states.

Duration: several class periods
Group Size: several teams of 2–4 students
Skills: observation, communication
Disciplines: history, geography, sociology, language arts, math
Key Vocabulary: state names and specific locations within the states
Materials: large U.S. map, game pieces, index cards/clue cards

**Procedure**

Prior to beginning game, copy information about locations within the United States, located at the end of this section, onto index cards.

1. Write RALLY on several cards with no state descriptions.
2. Divide the class into teams. Allow each team to develop their game piece and name their team. Game pieces can be 1/2 of a 3 × 5 index card decorated with a motorized-vehicle picture from a magazine. Each team should identify one person on the team to do each of the following: (a) select a clue card, (b) read the clue card from other team, (c) state aloud the answer to the question, (d) move the game piece on the map, (e) keep the clue cards of correctly answered questions.
3. Determine the order in which teams will play. Review the rules with the class.
4. The designee from Team 1 draws a clue card and, without looking at the card, passes it to the appropriate player on Team 2 to read aloud.
5. Team 1 has one minute to discuss the clue and decide on an answer. They may refer to the map if they wish.
6. If Team 1 answers the clue correctly, they may move their game piece to the location identified in their response.
7. Team 1 keeps their card if the question is answered correctly.
8. Team 2 now draws a clue card and passes it to the appropriate player on Team 3.
9. Team 2 uses the same procedure as Team 1. Play then continues to each team in turn.
10. If a team provides an incorrect response to a clue card, the card is placed randomly within the deck, and the team's game piece remains in the same place.
11. If a rally card is selected, the team may move to any place on the map without answering a question. Once all of the cards have been answered correctly, the team with the most correct responses wins.
12. If upon responding to a clue card a team ends up on the same state as another team, the first team must move their game piece to the Gulf of Mexico until they answer another clue card correctly.

**Extensions/Adaptations**

- Encourage students to develop clue cards to add to the game or to replace current clue cards.
- Questions can be developed by the students to relate to various countries around the world. Using a world map, the game can be played in the same way.
- Questions can be developed for a specific state. Using a state map, teams can "visit" different places in their state.
- Using road maps, have students use scale to determine distances between locations.

**Recommended Children's Books**

Gordon, Patricia. (1999). *Kids Learn America*. Williamson Publishing.
Guthrie, Woody. (1998). *This Land Is Your Land*. Little, Brown and Company.
Krull, Kathleen. (1997). *Wish You Were Here: Emily's Guide to the 50 States*. Bantam Books.
Leedy, Loreen. (1999). *Celebrate the 50 States*. Holiday House.
Miller, Millie. (2001). *United States of America: A State by State Guide*. Scholastic Books.
Rylant, Cynthia. (1998). *Tulip Sees America*. Scholastic Trade Books.

**Technology Resources**

geography.about.com/library/maps/blusa.htm: Atlas of U.S. states, territories, and cities as well as geographical and data information.
www.mapblast.com: Gives access to maps of user-specified regions.
maps.yahoo.com: Provides point-to-point driving directions and maps.

**Information for Clue Cards**

- This city is below sea level and was one of the first 20 states of the U.S. (New Orleans, LA)
- At one time people traveled from the Northeast to enjoy the relaxing, hot thermal waters of this city. (Hot Springs, AR)
- The first shot of the Civil War was fired in this city and state. (Charleston, SC)

- This southern capital city was burned during the Civil War. (Atlanta, GA)
- The home of country music and the country-music recording industry is located here. (Nashville, TN)
- The highest wind speeds ever clocked in the U.S. were at _____. (Mount Washington, NH)
- The Grand Tetons are located just outside this city. (Jackson, WY)
- This city is the home of the Golden Gate Bridge. (San Francisco, CA)
- This East Coast location is the site of the U.S. space-launch facilities. (Cape Canaveral, FL)
- This city is located on an island and is within the Acadia National Park. (Bar Harbour, ME)
- Yellowstone National Park is located just west of this city, which is named after a cowboy. (Cody, WY)
- The winter home of Barnum and Bailey Circus is located in this city. (Venice, FL)
- The center of the U.S. movie industry is located in _____. (Hollywood, CA)
- The U.S. Naval Academy is located in _____. (Annapolis, MD)
- The Meteor Crater and the Petrified Forest are located within 50 miles of ____. (Winslow, AZ)
- This state is known for sugar cane, pineapple, and volcanoes. The most popular city is visited by tourists who must arrive by plane or ship. (Honolulu, HI)
- The first atomic bomb was tested in the area of _____. (White Sands, NM)
- The U.S. Air Force Academy is located near the Garden of the Gods in ___. (Colorado Springs, CO)
- The U.S. Army Military Academy is located in _____. (West Point, NY)
- This is the oldest city in the Louisiana Purchase. (Natchitoches, LA)
- Mount Hood is located approximately 80 miles from this capital city. (Salem, OR)
- The first African-American pilots in the U.S. Army Air Corps were trained at _____. (Tuskegee, AL)

- This city is the northernmost city in the continental United States. (Barrow, AK)
- The Grand Canyon is located approximately 80 miles north of this city. (Flagstaff, AZ)
- A sister city in Canada has the same name. Both are located beside a very large waterfall. (Niagara Falls, NY)
- A large Civil War battle occurred in this city located on the bluffs above the Mississippi River. (Vicksburg, MS)
- Located on the shore of Lake Michigan, this large city is the home of O'Hare Airport. (Chicago, IL)
- The Operations Center for NASA is located here. (Houston, TX)
- Theodore Roosevelt National Park is south of Saskatchewan, Canada and 117 miles west of this city. (Bismarck, ND)
- Mt. Sunflower, the highest point in the state at the CO state line, is located due west of this state capital. (Topeka, KS)
- The capital city of the state divided by Lake Michigan and Lake Huron. (Lansing, MI)
- Lake Tahoe is located in the state where the capital city has the same name as a famous cowboy. (Carson City, NV)
- The home of the space needle is here. (Seattle, WA)
- The Great Salt Lake Desert is located to the west of this capital and largest city. (Salt Lake City, UT)
- This is the capital city of the smallest state. (Providence, RI)
- The Alamo is located in _____. (San Antonio, TX)
- This is the capital city of the state that is most well known for the potato industry. (Boise, ID)
- This city is located on a bay just south of Philadelphia, but in a different state. (Wilmington, DE)
- This Midwestern city is home to the annual Indy 500. (Indianapolis, IN)
- This is the capital city of the state that is bordered on the east by the Mississippi River and on the west by the Missouri River. (Des Moines, IA)
- This city is the location from which wagon trains left during the westward expansion. (St. Joseph, MO)
- This city in the bluegrass state is home to "The Derby." (Louisville, KY)

- This northeastern city was the home of the witch trials in the 1600s and 1700s. (Salem, MA)
- This four-word, hyphenated location is in the heart of Amish Country in Lancaster County. (Bird-In-The-Hand, PA)
- St. Paul and _____ are the twin cities in this state. (Minneapolis, MN)
- Glacier National Park is located just below the Alberta, Canada, border in the state with this, its largest city. (Billings, MT)
- This capital city is in the state in which Omaha is the largest city. (Lincoln, NE)
- The Wright brothers made the first successful airplane flight at this location. (Kitty Hawk, NC)
- This northeast coast city is named for the ocean by which it is bordered. (Atlantic City, NJ)
- Mount Rushmore is located immediately northeast of this city. (Rapids City, SD)
- The "Heart of Rock and Roll" is said to be located in ___. (Cleveland, OH)
- The Trail of Tears ended in the state in which this city is the capital city. (Oklahoma City, OK)
- General George Washington spent a very cold winter at this location. (Valley Forge, PA)
- A person must cross on the toll ferry across Lake Champlain to reach this state's largest city. (Burlington, VT)
- This city was the home of Thomas Jefferson. (Monticello, VA)
- This place was the birthplace of George Washington. (Mount Vernon, VA)
- The Tomb of the Unknown Soldier, the U.S. Capitol Building, and the Lincoln Memorial are located here. (Washington, DC)
- The state in which this city is the capital is well known for coal mining. (Charleston, WV)
- The capital of the state known as America's Dairy Land is _____. (Madison, WI)

## IMAGINARY ISLAND

In cooperative groups, students use encoding and decoding skills to develop a map of an imaginary island and incorporate scale, longitude and latitude, natural and manmade resources, prevailing winds, modes of travel, and other items related to the legend or map key.

Duration: 2–4 class periods

Group Size: individual or in pairs

Skills: problem solving, cooperative learning, analyzing, decision making, planning and designing, synthesis, application

Disciplines: geography, language arts, science, math, fine arts

Key Vocabulary: longitude, latitude, bay, peninsula, prevailing winds, natural resources, manmade resources, prime meridian, equator, continent, legend

Materials: writing materials, world maps (for resource), globes (for resource), crayons or markers

**Procedure**

*Part 1*

1. Draw the shape of the island. It may be any shape but must include one peninsula and one bay.
2. Indicate the four major directions on the map in the upper right corner.
3. Examine the world map or a globe and determine what coordinates will border the island. Be sure that you do not place the island on top of any existing landforms. Indicate the coordinates on the map.
4. Begin the legend by showing a scale of miles for the island.
5. Draw a mountain range that includes a mountain pass going from east to west across the island.
6. Show a city in the northern half of the island and one in the southern half of the island. Make one a seaport.
7. Show a railroad joining the two cities.
8. Indicate either one or two roads (or highways or streets) on the island.
9. Show three rivers, a lake, and a swamp on the island.
10. Place a third city somewhere on the map where you think a city should be located.

11. Show boundary lines that divide the island into two large countries and one small country.
12. Draw the lines of latitude and longitude (in addition to those that border the island) on the map.
13. Indicate the appropriate symbols used on the island in the legend.

## Part 2

1. With students, brainstorm types of information that would be needed by someone wishing to visit any one of the islands for which they have designed maps. Put this information on a chart for referral. Provide each student (or student pair) with a map that is not his or her own.
2. Students create tri-fold brochures (including illustrations and text) for each island, which include the information brainstormed as a class. Students share brochures and maps with the rest of class, focusing on location and description. Put maps, brochures, and a world map up as an interactive bulletin board. Students can use string or yarn to connect maps with locations on the world map.

## Extensions/Adaptations

- Have groups of students (3–4) construct maps on poster board.
- Provide an outline of a map and allow students to complete specific components with entire-class participation.
- Provide an outline of the laminated map on poster board as part of an interactive bulletin board. Place direction cards beside the board and allow students to complete using grease pencils or markers. This is erasable, once checked by the teacher.
- Design tourist Web pages for each island.
- Have students develop a slogan in a foreign language for the new island (see babelfish.altavista.digital.com/translate.dyn).
- Allow students to use reference materials to find out information about places located in the same geographic area as their own.
- Encourage students to be creative and create their own cultures to accompany their islands.

## Recommended Children's Books

Anno, M. (1997). *Anno's Journey*. Philomel.

Anno, M. (1999). *All in a Day*. Philomel.

Anno, M. (1998). *Anno's USA*. Sandcastle Books.

Hincks, G. (1997). *Rand McNally's around the World*. Rand McNally.

Leedy, Loreen. (2000). *Mapping Penny's World*. Henry Holt and Company Incorporated.

Lucas, D., & Veerman, D. (eds.) (1998). *106 Questions Children Ask about Our World*. Tyndale House Publishers.

Murphy, Stuart J. (2004). *Treasure Map*. Harper Collins.

National Geographic Society. (1994). *National Geographic's Picture Atlas of Our World*. Washington, DC.

## Technology Resources

www.immigration-usa.com/maps/abc_world_maps.html: Extensive collection of small maps of countries around the world including maps to print and color.

babelfish.altavista.digital.com/translate.dyn: Translates among major languages.

www.gsi.go.jp/ENGLISH/MAPS/VARIETIES/IMAGINARY/animap-e.html: A series of imaginary animal maps.

www.lib.utexas.edu/Libs/PCL/Map_collection/islands_oceans_poles: A collection of detailed maps of islands around the world.

## THE HOMESTEAD ACT

Students will measure an estimated acre and develop a plan for developing a 160-acre tract of land.

Duration: 2–4 class periods

Group Size: whole class, pairs, and small groups

Skills: analyzing, generalizing, planning, describing

Disciplines: history, geography, economics, mathematics, physical education

Key Vocabulary: The Homestead Act, homesteads, acre, tract, represent, house raising

Materials: flour, writing materials, crayons or markers, poster board or large construction paper

## Procedure

*Part 1*

1. Discuss the Homestead Act, including the following questions: Could African Americans own land? Could the Chinese? The Irish? Who could not own land? Why not? Check the following websites: www.pbs.org/weta/thewest/rescources/archives/five/homestead.htm and www.historyonthnet.com/Lessons/worksheets/american_west.htm (heading: "The Homestead Act of 1862").

2. Take the class outside and tell students that the task is to mark off a tract of land that would be an estimated one acre.

3. Mark a starting point. Place an object at this location.

4. From the starting point, walk 84 paces (about 164 children's giant steps) in a straight line.

5. Have someone stand at this point to mark the corner.

6. At this point, turn at a right angle and walk 84 more paces. Mark this corner with a person.

7. Walk another 84 paces at a right angle from the second person.

8. Walk the final 84 paces at a right angle from the third person.

9. Have the remainder of the students form the boundaries between points of the acre to provide a better visualization of one acre. Mark the entire area perimeter with flour and allow students time to circle the entire area to see better the approximate size of an acre. Ask questions such as the following: How long does it take to walk around the outside of an acre? How long does it take to walk diagonally from one corner of an acre to the other (i.e., northwest to southeast)? How long does it walk to walk from the northernmost side of the acre to the southernmost side?

10. Discuss how much bigger a 2-acre tract would be than this one. A 4-acre tract? A 100-acre tract?

11. Continue the discussion of the Homestead Act.

12. Once a person settled and farmed his or her land for five years, the final deed for the property was passed on to the person. The cost was $18.00 for each grant and eleven cents per acre. Have students determine the cost of acres as part of word problems.

Following are some examples:

a. You have bought a grant and now want to buy one acre of land. You have sixty-six cents. How much money would you have left over after you bought the acre?

b. You have $20.00. How much money would you need to buy the grant and three acres of land? Do you have any money left over? How much? Could you buy any more land with the amount you have left over? How much land could you buy?

c. If you wanted to pay for the grant for your land and buy one acre, how much money would you need?

*Part 2*

1. Discuss the term "house raising." Provide each student group of two or three with a large piece of construction paper or a piece of poster board. Tell them that the paper represents a one-acre tract of land. Together they are to draw ("raise") their cabin on their land. They should draw their cabin as well as any trees, fences, animals, and crops that would be on their land.

2. Put final homesteads on a bulletin board. Discuss how these homesteads could all be in a community but would be many miles apart.

**Extensions/Adaptations**

- Outline a one-acre tract on the playground with flour. Have students do the following: walk off a second acre, form the boundary on all sides by standing on top of the flour, use a measuring wheel to determine the size of the acre.

- Use Lincoln Logs, Legos, pretzel sticks, or twigs to cooperatively build a cabin.

- Visit a local cabin in the vicinity or have a guest speaker (builder) answer questions about log-cabin construction.

- Discuss the land and climate found in settlement areas: New Mexico, Nevada, Arizona, California. Which areas would be more conducive to growing certain kinds of crops? Obtain several soil samples and attempt to grow the same type of plant (crop/vegetable) in the different soils.

- Why is the Homestead Act not used today in the United States? Are there places where this kind of land development could work? Where? Why?
- Use a trashcan or other solid item for the starting point rather than having a student serve as the marker. Have all students walk the acre with you, having various ones stop along the way to form the corners. Use a nondiscriminative method of deciding who will mark corners (e.g., students who have birthdays in March).

## Recommended Children's Books

Chambers, Catherine E. (1998). *Log Cabin Home*. Troll Communications.
Foran, Jill. (2003). *Homesteading*. Weigle Publishers, Inc.
Isaacs, Sally Senzell. (2001). *Life on a Pioneer Homestead*. Heinemann Library.
Richardson, Arleta. (2001). *Prairie Homestead*. Cook Communication Ministries.
Stein, Richard Conrad. (1978). *The Story of the Homestead Act*. Children's Press.

## Technology Resources

www.pbs.org/weta/thewest/rescources/archives/five/homestead.htm: Basic information detailing the Homestead Act of 1862.
www.historyonthenet.com/Lessons/worksheets/american_west.htm: (heading: "The Homestead Act of 1862")—Discussion questions and content about the Homestead Act.
www.users.rcn.com/deeds/homestead.htm: A brief history of the Homestead Act of 1862 and descriptions of the people who became homesteaders.

# CHAPTER 4

# Individual Development and Identity

Make the most of yourself for that is all there is of you.

—Ralph Waldo Emerson

No bird soars too high if he soars with his own wings.

—William Blake

As students begin exploring how identity is shaped by culture, organizations, institutions, and other individuals, they begin to gain awareness of the expectations, values, and conventions of society. This awareness helps to develop their understanding of the societal forces that help shape how one grows as an individual. Students first begin to develop their identities within their personal social context of siblings, parents, and communities, with siblings and parents playing the primary roles. As they grow older, peers play an increasingly more significant role in the shaping of identity. Students begin to more closely examine and modify their own beliefs in relationship to those of their peers and others within their own culture and subculture.

Understanding the unique features of individual families and identifying and describing ways that ethnic, regional, and global cultures influence lives on a daily basis are necessary to promote an increased understanding of one's self and of others. This understanding will enable individuals to appreciate not only their own motivation, thought processes, and actions, but also those of others both similar to and different from themselves. The disciplines of anthropology and psychology provide contexts through which students can become more aware of the unique contributions of the various influences that help shape themselves and others.

## TRADING CARDS

Students will focus on characteristics unique to themselves and begin to become aware of their similarities to and differences from others.

Duration: 1 class period
Group Size: whole class
Disciplines: sociology, psychology, language arts, fine arts
Skills: describing, generalizing, classifying, evaluating, interpreting, analyzing
Key Vocabulary: uniqueness
Materials: index cards for each child, scissors, paste, photograph of each child

### Procedure

1. Either use a digital camera to photograph each child and print the photo or ask parents to provide a photograph of their child for classroom use.
2. Provide each student with an index card (5 × 8).
3. Have each student paste his or her photograph on one side of the card. On the back of the card, students write personal information related to name, birthday, birthplace, favorite sport, book, software, television show, color, hobbies, and so on.
4. Have students decorate the cards, focusing on an aspect unique to the individual.
5. Share and discuss cards with other students. Compare and contrast similarities and differences.
6. Laminate cards or cover them with clear contact paper. Keep as a set for students to use to do the following:

   • classify according to similarities, differences, and so on.
   • play card games—make pairs according to specific similarities (same favorite television show, book, birth month, etc.).
   • Alphabetize according to first or last name.

### Extensions/Adaptations

- Make cards on the first day of school to help students become better acquainted with each other and to enable the teacher to better know and understand individual students.
- Repeat the activity approximately one month before the school year ends. Discuss changes that have occurred during the year. Discuss additional changes that students predict will happen over the summer.

### Recommended Children's Books

Brown, Jeff. (2003). *Flat Stanley*. Harper Trophy.
Fine, Anne. (2002). *The Angel of Nutshell Road*. Egmont Children's Books.
Freeman, Don. (1977). *Dandelion*. Puffin Books.
Gilmore, Rachna. (2000). *Mina's Spring of Colors*. Fitzhenry and Whiteside.
Gliory, Debi. (1998). *The Snowchild*. Aladdin.
Halvorsen-Sehreck, Karen. (2001). *Lucy's Family Tree*. Tilbury House Publishers.
Payne, Lauren, & Rohling, Claudia. (1994). *Just Because I Am*. Free Spirit Publishing.
Pfister, M. (1992). *Rainbow Fish*. North-South Books.
Recorvits, Helen. (2003). *My Name is Yoon*. Frances Foster Books.
Walsh, Ellen Stoll. (1998). *For Pete's Sake*. Harcourt Brace.
Yangsook, Choi. (2003). *The Name Jar*. Dragonfly Books.

### Technology Resources

www.childparenting.about.com/cs/emotionalhealth/a/selfesteem2.htm: Things to do to help children build both self-esteem and a sense of uniqueness.
www.pbs.org/wholechild/providers/play.html: Fostering creativity in play to aid children in the development of their own unique talents.
www.cthistoryonline.org/classrm_lessplan_family.html: Students investigate two Connecticut families using photographs and text to develop an understanding of similarities and differences.

## GETTING TOGETHER WITH FRIENDS

Students will compare their current social activities with those of the past and will model several activities from a pioneer setting.

Duration: one class period
Group Size: whole class
Disciplines: sociology, psychology, history, philosophy, fine arts
Skills: describing, generalizing, classifying, evaluating, interpreting, analyzing
Key Vocabulary: socialization, entertainment, work
Materials: newsprint, variety of children's books (see references), markers, magazines, glue

## Procedure

1. Discuss socialization aspects: focus on different socialization activities dependent on the specific culture.
2. Select two or three stories or books that show socialization and work aspects of the pioneers.
3. With the class, construct a compare-and-contrast chart (on newsprint) that will show what their social life is like today as compared with pioneer times. Use pictures from magazines, as well as key words, to illustrate these comparisons.
4. On the chart, include descriptions of everyday events such as what they and the children of the past do/did for fun; where do/did they go; how do/did they get there; with whom do/did they socialize; how difficult is/was it to visit a friend, neighbor, or relative; what it is/was like to go shopping for food.
5. Place the chart on the wall in the classroom. Focus the discussion on the ideas of philosophy (values and beliefs), sociology (society), and psychology (human behavior) as the basis for why communities and individuals relied on one another more at this earlier time in history than currently.

## Extensions/Adaptations

- Use an agree/disagree chart, right-angle chart, or semantic map instead of the compare and contrast chart.
- Divide students into groups of 3–4 and provide each group with two books. Compare and contrast socialization and work between stories within the books. Place this information on a chart and share it with the rest of the class.

- Develop a bulletin board as a class that compares and contrasts socialization and work today and in the late 1700s and early 1800s. Use pictures from magazines and newspapers.
- Compare and contrast activities of boys and girls from today and pioneer times on a chart with three columns: Unique to Us, The Same—Then and Now, Unique to the Pioneers.

## Recommended Children's Books

Brown, Laurie Krasney. (2001). *How to be a Friend: A Guide to Making Friends and Keeping Them.* Little, Brown and Company.

Madonna. (2003). *The English Roses.* Viking Books.

McLerran, Alice. (2004). *Roxaboxen.* Harper Trophy.

Park, Barbara. (2002). *Junie B., 1st Grader.* Random House.

Shriver, Maria. (2002).*What's Wrong with Timmy?* Little, Brown and Company.

Tunis, Edwin. (2000). *Frontier Living: An Illustrated Guide to Pioneer Life in America Including Log Cabins, Furniture, Tools, Clothing, and More.* Lyon Press.

Whybrow, Ian. (2002). *Wish, Change, Friend.* Margaret McElderry Publishers.

## Technology Resources

www.linktolearning.com/pioneers/pioneers.htm: Pioneer life and social activities in upper Canada.

www.eagle.ca/~matink/themes/Pioneers/lessons.html: Pioneer lesson plans.

www.42explore2.com/pioneer.htm: Numerous links and webquests related to a variety of pioneer experiences.

## CREATING A FAMILY TREE

By simplifying the creation of a family tree, students more easily understand the concept of a family tree and are able to construct their own.

Duration: 2 class periods
Group Size: whole class and individuals
Disciplines: sociology, psychology, language arts, fine arts

Skills: describing, generalizing, classifying, evaluating, interpreting, analyzing

Key Vocabulary: uniqueness, genealogy, family tree

Materials: photographs, paper, drawing/writing materials, glue

## Procedure

1. Read *Me and My Family Tree* to the class. This book simplifies creating a family tree into steps that young children can easily understand.
2. Make a sample family tree for students using your own photos, illustrations, and words. Discuss how they can make one of their own by bringing photos from home, drawing pictures (as the girl in the story does), or putting small apple shapes on a tree with names on it.
3. Students decide how they each want to make their family tree; trees are constructed the following day (so those who want to use pictures can bring them in).

## Extensions/Adaptations

- Use other recommended books and produce a family tree that goes back at least one generation.
- Conduct genealogy searches online while constructing the family tree.
- Have students interview older relatives and record family stories. Transcribe stories and make illustrated family storybooks.

## Recommended Children's Books

Halvorsen-Sehreck, Karen. (2001). *Lucy's Family Tree*. Tilbury House Publishers.

Laden, Nina. (1997). *My Family Tree: A Bird's Eye View*. Chronicle Books.

Leedy, Lorraine. (1999). *Who's Who in My Family*. Sagebrush Education Resources.

Perl, Lila. (1999). *The Great Ancestor Hunt: The Fun of Finding Out Who You Are*. Sagebrush Educational Resources.

Sweeney, Joan. (2000). *Me and My Family Tree*. Dragonfly Books.

Wolfman, Ira. (2002). *Climbing Your Family Tree: Online and Off-line Genealogy for Kids*. Workman Publishing.

### Technology Resources

www.familytreemagazine.com/articles/oct01/kids.html: Tips and techniques for junior genealogists.

pbskids.org/wayback/family/tp.html: Helping children explore their own history.

www.homemadesimple.com/living/familytree.shtml: Family tree construction for younger children.

## THE POSITIVE VALUE OF DIFFERENCES

Students will begin to develop an awareness and understanding that differences among people have a positive value to society and that such differences add to the quality, interest, and value of life.

Duration: 2 class periods

Group Size: whole class and individuals

Disciplines: sociology, psychology, language arts, fine arts, philosophy

Skills: describing, generalizing, classifying, evaluating, analyzing

Key Vocabulary: characteristics

Materials: one piece of fruit (not an apple), an apple for each student in the class (apples should be of various sizes, shapes, colors) plus extras, knife

### Procedure

1. Place the selected piece of fruit where all students can see it. Discuss the obvious characteristics of the fruit (color, shape, size). Direct attention to the special characteristics of the fruit (scars, leaves, lopsidedness, etc.). Discuss how these things might have happened to the fruit.

2. Place apples on a table in front of the class (apples should not be "perfect"). Allow each student in the class to choose an apple.

Tell students to get to know their apple really well but to especially notice their apple's special characteristics.

3. Have them make up a story (with a beginning, middle, and end)
   about their apple and tell it to a friend. Allow the students to share
   their stories with the rest of the class. Direct the students to return
   their apples to the table in front of the class. Mix the apples up
   and ask the students to come back and find their apple. When they
   return to their seats, ask how they knew which apple was theirs
   (they will indicate things like color, size, shape, special features).

4. Discuss what this (the activity) has to do with people. Brainstorm
   a list of how people are different. Discuss why this is important.

5. Direct students (through questions) to summarize the importance
   of individual differences in people.

### Extensions/Adaptations

- For younger students, model the storytelling step about the initial
  piece of fruit prior to continuing the activity using individual apples.
- Generate lists about fruit characteristics in cooperative groups and
  then share these lists with the entire class.
- Generate a list of similarities as well as differences. Suggest that
  one way in which all people are similar is that they all have something special that they especially like about themselves, just as
  each apple has a star shape inside it. Cut each apple in half (don't
  cut the usual way, but through the center in the other direction).
  Let each child see the star inside their apple. While the students eat
  the apples, have them write in their journals about either the special "star" within them or a way in which they are different that
  makes them special.

### Recommended Children's Books

Benjamin, A. H. (2001). *Little Mouse and the Big Red Apple*. Tiger Tales.
Brown, T. (1995). *Someone Special, Just Like You*. Henry Holt & Co.
Fox, M. (1997). *Whoever You Are*. Harcourt.
Houghton, E. (2000). *The Crooked Apple Tree*. Barefoot Books.

Kissinger, K. (1994). *All the Colors We Are*. Redleaf Press.
Maestro, B. (1993). *How Do Apples Grow?* Harper Trophy.
Rickert, J. (1999). *Russ and the Apple Tree Surprise*. Woodbine House.
Riskind, M. (2001). *Apple is My Sign*. Sagebrush Bound.
Wellington, M. (2004). *Apple Farmer Annie*. Puffin Books.

## Technology Resources

www.zoomdinosaurs.com/graphicorganizers/: Features a variety of graphic organizers to aid in classification activities.

www.hhmi.org/coolscience/critters/critters.com: Classification of organisms for younger students.

www.projects.edtech.sandi.net/chavez/batquest/megabats.html: Classifying bats based on their individual differences.


## THE SAME AND DIFFERENT: CULTURAL CHARACTERISTICS

Students will compare cultural characteristics using selected categories as they explore similarities and differences of individuals.

Duration: 2–4 class periods

Group Size: whole class

Disciplines: sociology, psychology, language arts, mathematics, philosophy

Skills: observing, describing, generalizing, classifying, evaluating, analyzing

Key Vocabulary: similarities, differences, cultural characteristics, physical characteristics, natural characteristics

Materials: crayons/markers, drawing paper, chart paper


### Procedure

1. Have two volunteers stand in front of the rest of the class. The class will observe the students and generate ways in which the students are similar. Responses are written on chart paper. Ask leading questions to ensure that responses refer to cultural characterisitcs (games, holidays, foods, dwellings, etc.) as well as

physical/natural characteristics (eye color, hair color, height, weight, etc.)

2. As a class, select several (at least two) characteristics (both physical and cultural) that students can use as a basis of comparison. Create a "characteristics comparison chart" for the students to use.

3. Model interviewing techniques for the students. Pair students with other students they do not know well. Distribute a copy of the characteristics comparison chart for each student. Have students complete their chart during the interview.

4. Reconvene as a large group. Have individuals share information. Document information provided on similarities on a master comparison chart. Discuss as a group the following questions: How many of you celebrate the same holidays? How many of you have a favorite toy that is similar? How many of you enjoy _____ as your favorite food? Discuss that these are cultural characteristics and that some individuals who do not belong to a particular culture will still have some of these characteristics in common.

5. Repeat the process focusing on physical and cultural differences.

## Extensions/Adaptations

- Ask specific questions to direct comparisons: What language do you speak at home? How many of you celebrate Christmas? Kwaanza? Hanukah? Nothing? What is your favorite kind of food?
- Have students compare themselves to siblings or neighborhood friends. Bring data back to class and compare with the class composition of students.
- Use more characteristics depending on the grade level.
- Begin to discuss heredity as related to physical characteristics.
- Create a graph of the information for both similarities and differences of the class members.
- Discuss how cultural difference affect attitude toward life.

## Recommended Children's Books

Chamberlain, Margaret, & Greaves, Margaret. (1990). *Tattercoats*. Frances Lincoln Press.

Fox, Mem. (2001). *Whoever You Are*. Voyager Books.

Kates, Bobbi. (1992). *We're Different, We're the Same*. Random House.

Katz, Karen. (1999). *The Colors of Us*. Henry Holt and Company.

Viorst, Judith. (1974). *Rosie and Michael*. New York: Atheneum.

## Technology Resources

countrystudies.us/caribbean-islands/17.htm: The social and cultural characteristics of various Caribbean Islands are discussed.

www.michigan.gov/scope/0,1607,7-155-10710_10733_10740-43856--,00.html: A lesson on "How Does the Natural Environment Shape Cultural Characteristics?"

www.esu.edu/~mckenzie/readings/cultural_characteristics.htm: Features a discussion of cultural characteristics of eight countries.

# CHAPTER 5

# Individuals, Groups, and Institutions

All the world is a stage
And all the men and women merely players.
They have their exits and entrances;
Each man in his time plays many parts.

—William Shakespeare

Because of the influences that institutions, including churches, schools, governmental agencies, and social groups, have on the individual, students should become aware of how institutions and groups are formed, the people who influence and maintain or change them, and how these groups and institutions can exert influence over individuals. Opportunities to explore and discuss how various institutions and groups can and do influence students personally must be incorporated into the curriculum if this awareness is to be encouraged. An understanding of these influences can lead individuals to a greater self-determination through increased understanding of self and how one's cultural identity is influenced by surrounding institutions. Identifying the roles students play as individuals in families or group situations is best addressed through the disciplines of anthropology, history, political science, psychology, and sociology. The learning that occurs as a result of activities related to these areas will lead to the later topics of how institutions change over time, how institutions and groups promote conformity or nonconformity, and how social norms are the results of outside influences.

## EXPERIENCING THE LEGAL SYSTEM

As an introduction for students to the trial process, students will participate in a trial simulation using a well-known fairy tale that reflects current legal issues.

Duration: 2–3 class periods
Group Size: entire class or 2 groups
Disciplines: political science, language arts, civics
Skills: describing, evaluating, interpreting, inferring, predicting, analyzing, deducing, problem solving, cooperative learning
Key Vocabulary: jury, prosecutor, defense, attorney, brief, hostile witness, burden of proof, reasonable doubt, bailiff, verdict, court clerk
Materials: writing materials

### Procedure

1. Students read the story *The Snow Queen*.
   a. younger readers: Anderson, H. C. (1989). *The Snow Queen*. North South Books.
   b. older readers: Vinge, J. D. (1992). *The Snow Queen*. Warner Books.
2. Assist students in identifying the issues about which the Snow Queen could be put on trial (distribution of a controlled substance to a minor; false imprisonment—psychological or physical; child abuse/neglect). Discuss the story, focusing on items such as main characters, story line, and key facts of the conflict. Brainstorm diverse perspectives.
3. Assign (or solicit volunteers) to act as the Snow Queen, defense attorney, prosecuting attorney, judge, Gerta, Grandmother, Hobgoblin, Kye (and others as decided upon), and court clerk.
4. Discuss rules and terminology as needed: the jury members cannot speak during the trial—they should write down questions and ask the appropriate person later; effective questions to witnesses include Yes/No response questions; responses must be fact rather than opinion.

5. Using a trial format (see following section) based on a real-life trial and guidelines (see following section), involve students in the trial process.
6. Debrief students following the reading of the verdict. Discuss the following issues: Why is it important to hear both sides? What does the judge do? How is the jury important? Why can't lawyers' comments be used since they are the ones who really know the client on trial? If you can't use what the lawyers say to determine guilt or innocence, why do they have opening statements and closing arguments?

## Trial Format

1. Attorneys develop opening statements that explain what they plan to present to the court, what they plan to prove, and why. Defense and prosecuting attorneys decide who will be called to the witness stand.
2. Trial procedure: prosecution presents its opening statement first, then the defense presents its opening statement; prosecution calls each of its witnesses, and after each witness, the defense attorney has the opportunity to cross-examine; once the prosecutor has called all of its witnesses to the stand, and after each witness has been cross-examined, the defense attorney calls its witnesses to the stand, and the prosecutor is able to cross-examine; after all witnesses have testified, both attorneys present closing arguments, what they feel has or has not been proven, how, and why.
3. The prosecutor presents first, then the defense.
4. The jurors are then instructed by the judge to weigh all the evidence and are reminded that they can only base their decisions on what they have heard from witnesses, not on statements given by the attorneys. The jury deliberates (in front of the class provides more opportunity for discussion later) and then gives the judge the verdict to announce.

## Guidelines

1. Allow various jury members to work with defense and prosecuting attorneys to develop opening statements.

2. Have jury members identify a list of questions they would like to hear asked by either of the attorneys during the trial.
3. Assign some students to serve as assisting attorneys or legal aides.
4. Jury members should take notes to assist with deliberations.
5. It is important to have as many students as possible involved in the entire procedure. It is equally important to discuss issues, verdicts, and trial process following the trial in order to have an effective learning experience rather than just a fun activity.

## Extensions/Adaptations

- Use simpler stories/fairy tales (see the following section, "Recommended Children's Stories").
- Limit trial to address one issue.
- Allow an adult (staff member, parent, older student, another teacher) to serve as judge.
- Produce tangible evidence for attorneys to use and jury members to see (e.g., police report, doctor's report).
- Choose a problem that is relevant in terms of the age, concerns, and interests of the students.
- Allow students to use current happenings within the local and global community as a basis for trial-issue selection.
- Consult with a local law-enforcement agency and have a guest speaker come to class to familiarize students with procedure and terminology.
- Discuss trial processes in other countries and how they are similar to or different from the U.S. process.
- Compare trial processes from different time periods in history with today.
- Focus on how science and technology have affected the evidence presented to today's jurors.

## Recommended Children's Stories

| Fairy Tale/Story | Legal Issues |
| --- | --- |
| Goldilocks and the Three Bears | breaking and entering |
| 101 Dalmatians | stealing |

| | |
|---|---|
| The Three Little Pigs | murder/manslaughter; burglary; loitering; cruelty to animals |
| Jack and the Beanstalk | stealing; criminal mischief; trespassing |
| Three Billy Goats Gruff | harassment; blocking a highway; disorderly conduct; trespassing |
| Little Red Riding Hood | burglary; trespassing; criminal impersonation; destruction of property |
| Cinderella | child abuse; impersonation; kidnapping |
| Caps for Sale (Slobodkina) | stealing; harassment; neglect of duties |
| Why Mosquitoes Buzz in People's Ears | inciting to riot; harassment; disorderly conduct |
| Rapunzel | trespassing; child abuse; kidnapping |
| The Emperor's New Clothes | inciting to riot; fraud; blocking a roadway |
| Snow White | attempted murder; loitering; child abuse; trespassing; abuse of an illegal substance |
| Hansel and Gretel | kidnapping; desertion; harboring a runaway |
| The Twelve Dancing Princesses | trespassing; fraud; assault |
| The Ant and the Grasshopper | dereliction of duty |
| The Wizard of Oz | intent to cause bodily harm; impersonation; manslaughter |
| The Lion King | impersonation; fraud |

## Recommended Children's Books

Flanagan, Alice. (1998). *Day in Court with Mrs. Tronk*. Scholastic Library Publishing.

Leppard, Lois. (1996). *Maudie and the Courtroom Battle*. Sagebrush Educational Resources.

## Technology Resources

www.courts.state.wi.us: Structure and functioning of the Wisconsin Court System (typical of U.S. state systems).

www.judicial.state.ia.us/students/misc.asp: Contains a student summary of the judicial branch of the U.S. government.

www.usdoj.gov/usao/eousa/kidspage/index.html: How a courtroom works (version for children).

www.saccourt.com/geninfo/public_educ/court_tours/court_tours.asp: Describes what to expect on a court tour including "dos" and "don'ts."

## THE ASSEMBLY LINE

Through working on the construction of a product, students will identify and describe factors related to cooperation and lack of cooperation.

Duration: 1–2 class periods

Group Size: several groups of 3–5

Disciplines: economics, history, fine arts, math

Skills: describing, generalizing, classifying, evaluating, interpreting, inferring, hypothesizing, analyzing

Key Vocabulary: cottage industry, assembly line, division of labor, specialization, quality control

Materials: clown patterns (1 for each group), crayons, paper, scissors, pencils, glue

### Procedure

*Part 1*

Select a pattern for students to assemble individually. Allow a set amount of time so that everyone will have at least one completed item, possibly more. Keep these to post in the room at a later time.

*Part 2*

1. Discuss the terms assembly line, division of labor, and specialization. Focus on the cooperative nature of an assembly line. Talk about examples of assembly-line work and products.
2. Divide the class into several groups of three to five.
3. Identify the guidelines for constructing the pattern. For example, all clown faces must have the following: (a) 2 blue eyes, (b) or-

ange curly hair, (c) round green nose, (d) red smiling mouth. Stress that all clowns should look alike.

4. Identify a job for each person in the group. Model the strategy of finishing a task and passing the clown face to the next person to do his/her job. Tell the groups when to begin. Allow an appropriate amount of time (minutes) for the groups to work on their products (clown faces). Identify when to stop. Each person should focus on his or her job only. Completed clown faces should be put in a pile.

## Part 3

1. Discuss: working separately and together, the need for each person to do his or her job well to obtain a quality product, what happens when someone does not do his or her job.

2. Display the assembly-line products. Discuss how each group completed its task by comparing and contrasting the end results of each method of assembly, the benefits and limitations of each method of assembly, and the different types of items that best fit an assembly line and those that it would be more appropriate to construct individually.

3. Questions for discussion could include the following: What made one group work together better than other groups? What were some advantages of working by oneself the day before? What were some disadvantages of working together (or by oneself)? Who set the pace in the group work?

## Extensions/Adaptations

- Change the item to be assembled based on the age, interests, or unit of study of the class. Focus more on the competitive nature of the individual groups than on the completed product.

- Specify more specific roles (for example, a penguin pattern): (a) tracer—traces the pattern; (b) body cutter—cuts out the pattern; (c) colorer—colors black and white body parts; (d) features cutter—cuts out the eyes, feet, and beak; (e) attacher—glues on eyes, feet, and beak; and (f) quality control—examines each penguin and identifies each as acceptable or unacceptable. (Place products in a pile for each.)

- Provide a task to each group, but do not assign jobs. Allow groups to organize themselves as they see fit.
- Stress that the more a "company" produces, the more money it can make. Focus on the concepts of speed and stress when working on an assembly line. Discuss the need for each person to do his or her job well to obtain a quality product, the financial impact on the company when quality control "pulls" items from the end result because they have not been done well, and what will happen to someone working on an assembly line who does not produce quality work. Provide one group with higher quality materials than the others, and discuss the impact of inferior materials on the end product.
- Omit part 1 and on one day have some groups working as an assembly line while others work individually (focus on cottage industry vs. division of labor related to the Industrial Revolution).

### Recommended Children's Books

Hamper, Ben. (1992). *Rivethead: Tales from the Assembly Line*. Warner Books.

Weitzman, David. (2002). *How Henry Ford Built a Legend*. Crown Books.

Woods, Samuel G. (1999). *Chocolate: From Start to Finish*. Blackbirch Marketing.

Woods, Samuel G. (1999). *Crayons: From Start to Finish*. Blackbirch Marketing.

Woods, Samuel G. (1999). *Sneakers: From Start to Finish*. Blackbirch Marketing.

### Technology Resources

us.mms.com/us/about/history/story/: View a history lesson on chocolate and the manufacture of a popular candy.

People.clemson.edu/~pammack/lec323/assemblyline.htm: A brief explanation of the history of the assembly line with links.

www.ideafinder.com/history/inventions/story002.htm: The first moving assembly line in print and photograph form.

## GROUP CHARACTER TRAITS

Students will become aware of and evaluate specific character traits that are desirable when working with others and that are needed for specific jobs.

Duration: 1 class period
Group Size: whole group or small group
Disciplines: sociology, psychology, language arts
Skills: describing, generalizing, classifying, evaluating, inferring, analyzing
Key Vocabulary: traits, characteristics, help wanted
Materials: help-wanted ads, chart paper/overhead

**Procedure**

1. Model for students an interview situation in which you are asked the question, "Other than on-the-job training and going to school, what kinds of things would help a person do a good job of being a teacher?" Replies could be patience, flexibility, sense of humor, knowledge of content, and so on. Begin a list on chart paper with a particular job at the beginning of the column and each characteristic listed below the job.

2. Have students interview adults by asking the same question, substituting the adult's job for the teacher's. Compile the information on the chart. Have students speculate as to characteristics needed for any jobs not addressed that are of interest to the students.

3. Examine the lists and choose the ten characteristics that occur most frequently. Make a class chart of these characteristics.

4. Ask students to examine specific help-wanted ads and identify how the lack of one or more of the ten traits would affect a person's ability to do the job. Discuss how this set of traits addresses a particular group of people. Apply the use of the traits in various situations: when using the library, attending a concert, and the like. Discuss how any, all, or some of the character traits can help a group avoid potential problems.

### Extension/Adaptation

Leave the lists up. During the year, refer to the lists when problems arise during group activities. Have students identify characteristics that might have helped avoid the problem and that could help alleviate the problem. When projects are successfully completed during class time, have students identify the traits that were in operation.

### Recommended Children's Books

Flanagan, A. (1997). *Ms. Murphy Fights Fires*. Scholastic Library.
Glassman, Peter. (2003). *My Dad's Job*. Simon & Schuster Children's Books.
Hayward, Linda. (2001). *Day in the Life of a Doctor*. DK Publishing, Inc.
Hazeu, B. (1992). *Mommy's Office*. Macmillan Children's Books.
Kiefer, Jeanne. (2003). *Jobs for Kids*. Millbrook Press.
Marques, Eva, Sorensen, Carol, & Schulman, David. (1997). *100 Jobs for Kids and Young Adults*. Wisechild Press.
Reeves, Diane, Bryan, Gayle, & Bond, Nancy. (2001). *Career Ideas for Kids Who Like Music and Dance*. Facts on File Press.
Spinelli, E. (1993). *Boy Can He Dance*. Simon & Schuster Children's Books.

### Technology Resources

www.girlpower.gov/girlarea/sciencetech/jobs/index.htm: Descriptions of science and technology jobs for girls.
stats.bls.gov/k12/html/edu_over.htm: Career information for kids.
www.washburn.k12.il.us/neff/careers/careers.htm: Information on careers in many fields.

## WHAT IS FAIR?

By providing an unfair situation to introduce the concept of justice, students will become aware of possible solutions for problems and the ideas of fair and unfair.

Duration: 3–4 class periods
Group Size: entire class with subgroups
Disciplines: psychology, language arts

Skills: describing, evaluating, interpreting, inferring, predicting, analyzing, problem solving
Key Vocabulary: justice, fairness
Materials: as needed for self-determined situations

## Procedure

1. Construct a hypothetical situation to share with the class that identifies some specific aspect they will not be able to do or enjoy that all other classes will (e.g., a piece of playground equipment is off-limits to them, and the class must use other equipment until further notice; no music or art classes until everyone in the entire class makes a particular grade on an identified assignment; reduction in the amount of time for recess). Discuss the concept of fair and unfair related to the identified issues. Are there instances when something seems fair to one person but not to another? When? Under what circumstances?
2. Have groups of students identify situations they have seen (in various places such as the lunchroom, playground, mall, etc.) where they believe unfair practices exist. Discuss how sometimes things that seem unfair can be fair.
3. Read *Alexander Who Used to Be Rich Last Sunday*. Have students role-play the story. Create a classroom chart that outlines each instance in the story and identify whether each is fair and why or why not. Examine each instance from the points of view of both Alexander and the other individuals involved.
4. Compare and contrast why some "things" are fair in one instance but not in another.

## Extensions/Adaptations

- Over a several-day period, divide the class into groups, with some groups receiving more preferential treatment than other groups. For example, provide a "treat" for students, but don't have enough for all groups to participate; divide the class into two groups for a game, with one group having students that will be more able to complete the activity successfully; give two groups an independent-activity period (art, games, computer, etc.) while the other groups are given worksheets or structured activities.

* Continue this until the students begin to see and comment on the inequity of the situations (try for a three-day minimum). As a group, discuss feelings, emotions, and actions as a result of the experiences. Discuss the concept of fair and unfair related to the identified issues. Are there instances when something seems fair to one person but not to another? When? Under what circumstances? Compare responses from when the situation was hypothetical and from instances where the students were actually affected by the situation. How did this change the way they felt? Generate a list of comments and possible solutions. Conclude by discussing whether justice and fairness can occur for all people at all times.

### Recommended Children's Books

Berry, Jay. (1987). *Every Kid's Guide to Overcoming Prejudice and Discrimination*. Scholastic Library.

Cherry, Lynn. (1990). *The Great Kapok Tree: A Tale of the Amazon Rain Forest*. Voyager Books.

Couric, Katie. (2000). *The Brand New Kid*. Doubleday.

Derold, Shane, & Letzig, Michael. (1997). *The Crayon Box That Talked*. Random House.

Loewen, Nancy, & Wesley, Omarr. (2002). *No Fair!: Kids Talk About Fairness*. Picture Window Books.

Seskin, Steve, Shamblin, Allen, & Dibley, Glen. (2002). *Don't Laugh at Me*. Tricycle Press.

Viorst, J. (1999). *Alexander Who Used to Be Rich Last Sunday*. Econoclad Books.

### Technology Resources

www.abanet.org/publiced/lawday/schools/lessons/handout_fair.html: An American Bar Association K–3 lesson on "Fairness and Equal Treatment."

www.goodcharacter.com/pp/fairness.html: A brainstorming activity for children about fairness.

tigger.uic.edu/~lnucci/MoralEd/practices/unitpeers.html: A lesson plan concerning peers and fairness.

## CYCLICAL BREAKDOWN

By physically forming an interconnected circle, students will demonstrate and gain awareness of the effects of a breakdown in a group,
community, or institution.

Duration: 1 class period
Group Size: several groups of 3–5
Disciplines: science, sociology, economics
Skills: describing, generalizing, evaluating, interpreting, inferring,
   hypothesizing, analyzing
Key Vocabulary: cycle, cyclical, breakdown, interconnected, depen-
   dence
Materials: rubber ball, space

### Procedure

*Part 1*

Prior to the activity, select two students and direct each to not follow
through on the action of the circle when you give a predetermined signal. Other class members should not know this is going to occur. Tell
the two students this will not take place until the second round of the
activity.

1. Have students form a circle with each person holding the hand of
   the person on either side of him or her, with the teacher being one
   of the members in the circle.
2. The teacher (or a designated student) squeezes the hand of the
   person to his or her left or right (not both). That person then
   squeezes the hand of the next, who squeezes the hand of the next,
   and so on until the squeeze is returned to the person who initiated
   the motion. Discuss the need for all to participate for the initial
   action to continue to the desired conclusion.
3. In the second round, use the signal to indicate to the two preselected
   students that they should not participate during this round (however,
   they remain in place and pretend they are). Repeat the previous

procedure. When students begin questioning why their hand has not been squeezed, the "planted students" can deny that they did not squeeze the person's hand next to them. Discuss what happens when there is a breakdown in communication among members of a group, what can be done to determine where the breakdown occurred, and what can be attempted to "fix" the problem.

*Part 2*

1. Stand in a circle with each person's arms in front of them, palms up. (The circle should be close, with shoulders almost touching). Place a ball in one person's hand. The ball is passed from person to person by passing the ball along from hand to hand or by tossing the ball to the next person. After the ball has gone around the complete circle, have everyone place one hand behind his or her back. Continue passing the ball. What happens when certain components of the group (one hand each) are removed? Things can continue to work, but what are the problems? How is this similar to things that happen in our lives when we are trying to work with other people?

2. Identify each person in the circle as a specific component from an organization: 1 principal, 2 custodians, 5 teachers, 3 secretaries, 15 students. Discuss how each person listed has a job to do. Return to the circle, standing close enough that shoulders are touching. Tell all teachers to step out of the circle. Discuss the following questions: What would happen if the teachers didn't come to work? Who "takes up the gap" left by the people who have left? Would the job of the teachers get accomplished? If so, how? How well? If not, why not? Return teachers to the circle and repeat by removing another component. Discuss the importance of certain members of the group over others. What determines importance in a group? Repeat using other examples such as consumer, salesperson, buyer, farmer, milk, cows, barn.

3. Discuss the following: what the group expresses as the essential components of a group so that all members work effectively together, how members of the group must work together, and attitudes of group members if certain members do not do their assigned tasks.

## Extensions/Adaptations

You can perform science adaptations using circuits, habitat, and electrons/protons/neutrons.

## Recommended Children's Books

Cadoto, Michael, et. al. (1997). *Keepers of the Earth: Native American Stories and Environmental Activities for Children*. Fulcrum Publishing.

Fleischman, Paul. (1999). *Westlandia*. Candlewick Press.

Foreman, Michael. (1990). *One World*. Arcade Publishing.

Fredricks, Tony. (2002). *Under One Rock: Bugs, Slugs, and Other Ughs*. Dawn Publications.

Green, Jen. (1999). *A Dead Log*. Crabtree Publishing.

Grooms. Steve. (1999). *Return of the Wolf*. Northword Press.

Metzger, Steve, & Wilhelm, Hans. (2000). *Dinofours, My Seeds Won't Grow*. Scholastic.

Petrash, Carol, & Cook, Donald. (1992). *Earthways: Simple Environmental Activities for Young Children*. Sagebrush Education Resources.

## Technology Resources

www.michigan.gov/scope/0,1607,7-155-13481_13487_13490-38720-,00.html: An activity stressing the interdependence of organisms.

atozteacherstuff.com/lessons/GreatKapokTree.shtml: A lesson about the Great Kapok Tree and the interdependence of organisms.

www.biokids.umich.edu/projects/activities.html: An activity illustrating how life-forms are interdependent.

# CHAPTER 6

# Power, Authority, and Governance

> My country owes me nothing. It gave me, as it gives every boy and girl, a chance. It gave me schooling, independence of action, opportunity for service and honor.
>
> —Herbert C. Hoover

Power, authority, and governance focuses on the key areas of government, history, law, and political science, which are necessary to promote an understanding of civics education in younger children. By providing students with opportunities to gain understanding of the issues and content related to such areas as the role of the government, values and ethics of democracy, the constitution, the relationship of the United States and other world nations, and the roles of citizens, educators can promote responsible participation in political life by informed and competent citizens committed to the basic principles of constitutional democracy. Student experiences that foster understanding of the development of power, authority, and governance structures within their own country, as well as within other countries comprising the world community, will assist in the growth of civic competence.

The goals addressed through these endeavors include the following: providing an understanding of the principles, concepts, and beliefs that constitute the basis for and guide the administration of justice in our society; promoting positive attitudes toward the protection and application of our fundamental freedoms and toward the accomplishment of citizenship responsibilities; encouraging the application of basic skills and higher-order thinking in day-to-day decision making; and assisting in the development of a willingness and capability to resolve conflicts through nonviolent means.

## IF YOU WERE IN CHARGE OF THE WORLD

Through modeling, students will develop a new version of a poem, focusing on authority by taking charge of the world in an effort to improve conditions at a local, state, regional, national, or global level.

Duration: 1–2 class periods
Group Size: full class, individually or in pairs
Disciplines: language arts, ecology, sociology
Skills: describing, generalizing, classifying, evaluating, analyzing
Key Vocabulary: power, authority, (others as needed for various grade levels)
Materials: copy of poem "If I Were in Charge of the World" for each child, writing materials

**Procedure**

*Part 1*

1. Read verse one with students. Discuss with students the purpose of verse one (things the person writing the poem would cancel if that person were in charge of the world).
2. Discuss some things in the world that students would like to cancel if they were in charge.
3. Read verse two. Ask students what verse two is about (things of which there would be more).
4. Read verse three. Ask students what verse three is about (things that wouldn't exist in the world).
5. Read verse four. Ask students what verse four is about (things we wish existed in the current world).
6. Brainstorm a list of issues and problems of which students are aware. Students model their own poems based on the format of this poem. Share completed poems among participants.

7. Discuss ideas suggested in poems: Which are realistic? About which could we write to our representatives? Which would be difficult to implement? What does authority mean? What is power? Who are some people we know who have authority or power? Over what do these people have authority? What is something over which each of you has power or authority?

*Part 2*

1. Extend the lesson into a second day. At the end of the first day ask the following questions: Who are some people you know of (but don't know personally) who have authority? Over what do these people have authority? Put list on board for use on second day.
2. Discuss people listed from the previous day. Introduce people from other countries who are considered to have power or authority. Discuss differences in power depending upon a country's government.

**Extensions/Adaptations**

- Students can read each verse either aloud or silently, but there must be discussion following the reading of each verse.
- The impact of the poem seems to be better if the verses are reviewed one at a time rather than reading the entire poem at once.
- This activity can easily be connected with any environmental topic and ways students can improve the environment. It can be extremely useful for students to exercise some power over their environment by doing some simple environmental projects such as cleaning up a playground, planting landscaping plants or trees, promoting conservation of resources within the community via a poster project, and so on.
- Write a group poem, with the teacher writing on chart paper and students contributing poem content.
- For older students, individual, paired, or small-group writing (to encourage cooperative learning) will work.
- When writing as a group, poem verses should begin, "If we were in charge . . ."

- *Brown Bear, Brown Bear, What Do You See? And Polar Bear, Polar Bear, What Do You Hear?* can be adapted for any number of topics such as, "Mr. President, Mr. President, what do you hear?" "Teacher, teacher, what do you see?" "Policeman, policeman, . . ." and so on.
- Modeling of *Quick as a Cricket* can be used to reflect character traits of specific people.

### Recommended Children's Books

Bender, Robert. (2000). *Lima Beans Would Be Illegal.* Dial Books for Young Readers.

Martin, B., Jr. (1996). *Brown Bear, Brown Bear, What Do You See?* New York: Holt and Company.

Martin, B., Jr. (1991). *Polar Bear, Polar Bear, What Do You Hear?* New York: Holt and Company. (Grades K–1)

Viorst, J. (1981). "If I Were In Charge of the World," "Since Hanna Moved Away," "Remember Me," "Learning." In *If I Were In Charge of the World and Other Worries.* New York: Simon and Schuster, Aladdin Paperbacks.

Wood, A. (1982). *Quick as a Cricket.* Child's Play International Ltd.

### Technology Resources

www.kidsvotingusa.org/family/online.asp: A wish site where students may read and add their wishes for the world.

www.wildgear.com/stories/ricebowl.html: A children's story of traditional values and wishing.

www.poetry4kids.com/: An instructional site about poems for children.

### FIELD TRIP TO THE WHITE HOUSE

Students will take a virtual field trip of the White House and describe content and concepts that they see and learn.

Duration: 1–2 class periods
Group Size: individual or pairs and entire class
Disciplines: political science, language arts, geography

Skills: describing, generalizing, classifying, interpreting

Key Vocabulary: similarities, comparisons, the White House, Venn diagram, virtual field trip

Materials: Internet access, writing materials, crayons or markers, U.S. map

## Procedure

*Part 1*

1. Locate Washington, D.C., on the map. Discuss the White House as the residence of the president of the United States.
2. Draw a Venn diagram (two overlapping circles) on the board or on chart paper.
3. Tell students the comparison will be between the White House and houses in which people other than the president and his family live. Brainstorm ways in which the White House and students' houses are alike and different and place information in the appropriate place on the Venn diagram. Accept all answers as the children provide them. Leave diagram up for students' reference. Tell students they will be visiting the White House to collect more information so they can place more comparisons and similarities on the diagram. Tell students that all of their assumptions about the White House may or may not be true and that they will support their ideas through the virtual field trip.

*Part 2*

1. Have students fold an 11 × 18-inch sheet of paper so that there are six sections. In each section, write one of these headings: Location, White House Kids, Our President, White House Pets, History, Write the President.
2. Have students access the White House on the Internet, at www.whitehouse.gov, and click on "White House for Kids."
3. Allow students sufficient time to explore the White House. Information related to each section can be added by students to the chart through key words, brief descriptions, complete sentences, or illustrations with captions. Have students turn the paper over and complete the following information: locate four rooms in the

White House, label each room, and draw a picture of an item that can be found in each room.

## Part 3

1. Review information gathered on the field-trip guide. Discuss how a field-trip guide helped them focus on the important information they needed to find. Refer to the Venn diagram. Have students identify additional information to place on the diagram.
2. Have students correct or replace information that was previously placed on the diagram that they have now identified as being incorrect or incomplete.

## Extensions/Adaptations

- Have students write a collaborative story (or individual stories), "If I Lived in the White House." This can be done from varying points of view: president, first lady, or daughter or son of the president.
- Construct a virtual field-trip guide for the Senate (www.senate .gov).
- Have students identify each room and identify a significant event that happened in each room.
- A field-trip guide can be constructed by students: use the front of one 8.5 × 11-inch sheet of paper for item one and the backside for item two.
- Construct virtual field trips to locations outside the United States: Buckingham Palace, 10 Downing Street, Red Square, and the like.

## Recommended Children's Books

Barnes, Peter, & Barnes, Cheryl. (1998). *Woodrow, the White House Mouse.* Vacation Spot Publishing.

Fleming, Candace. (1999). *A Big Cheese for the White House.*

Harness, Cheryl. (1997). *Ghosts of the White House.* Simon and Schuster.

Roosevelt, Anna. (2000). *Scamper: The Bunny Who Went to the White House.* The Wooster Book Company.

Thomsen, Steve. (1989). *The White House.* Capstone Press.

Van Wie, Nancy Ann. (1994). *A White House Tour.* Max's Publications.

Waters, Kate. (1992). *The Story of the White House.*

**Technology Resources**

www.whitehouse.gov/kids/traditions: A site where children can learn about White House traditions.
www.whitehouse.gov/kids/tours/: An online tour of the White House.
www.whitehouse.gov/kids/history/: A history of the White House.

## CHOOSING A LEADER

Students use anonymous attribute cards in conjunction with the criteria for president of the United States to select the three most- and one least-qualified individuals from the card population.

Duration: 1–2 class periods
Group Size: student pairs or small groups
Disciplines: history, philosophy, political science, sociology, language arts, civics
Skills: describing, generalizing, classifying, interpreting, inferring, communicating, evaluating, predicting, analyzing
Key Vocabulary: natural-born citizen, candidate, attribute, qualifications
Materials: writing materials, KWL chart, index cards

**Procedure**

1. Construct a KWL chart before beginning the topic (K—what students Know, W—what students Want to know, L—what students Learn during the activities). Brainstorm and discuss with students all the information they believe they know to be true about how a country elects its leader. All responses should be placed under the K category. Ask questions such as the following: How does voting take place? Who can vote? Who can't vote? Why do countries need leaders? (Why do we need a president?) Why do presidential elections happen every four years? What do presidents do? What is necessary for a person to run for the office of president?
2. Continue brainstorming and have students identify things they think they may know (or that they don't know) but that they would like to know. Place this information under the W column of the chart.

3. Begin constructing a word wall that focuses on words related to the election process and add to the wall throughout the study of elections.

4. Divide students into small groups. Groups individually brainstorm a list of qualifications that they feel a person should have to be considered for the office of the president. Each group should keep a written list of their qualifications. Groups share their lists with the rest of the class. Discuss whether any of the qualifications listed should be considered in selecting a presidential candidate. If any of the following items are not mentioned, discuss appropriate items with the class: religion, gender, current marital status, ethnicity, character, military service, educational background, physical health, previous occupations, number of children, number of times married or divorced, felonies or misdemeanors, personality, physical appearance.

5. Share with the students the three criteria necessary for a person to be considered for the presidency (natural-born citizen, U.S. resident for 14 years prior to presidential election, at least 35 years of age).

6. Have students generate a list of people whom they believe would be good candidates for becoming president of the United States. Suggestions can be drawn from such arenas as history, politics, entertainment, and so on. Place the names of all suggestions in a "hat" and allow each pair of students in the class to draw one name. Student pairs will be responsible for locating information on the assigned person related to marital status, number of children, religion, occupation, college degree, and any other items the students feel should be important.

7. After collecting the information, each student set develops two index cards, one with only the information to be provided to the remainder of the class, and the other with the information and the name of the person. Examples are as follows:

**Card 1**
Marital Status: married
Children: 2 adopted
Religion: Episcopalian
Occupation: farmer; soldier
College: no degree

**Card 2**

George Washington, 1789–1797

Nicknamed: Father of His Country

Married: Martha Dandridge Custis

Children: 2 adopted

Religion: Episcopalian

Occupation: farmer; soldier

College: no degree

Other Information: governmental positions: member of VA House of Burgesses, member of Continental Congress, chairman of the Constitutional Convention; notable events: Judiciary Act specifying the number of federal courts and judges; Supreme Court first met; Bill of Rights; Established Post Office and New York Stock Exchange; Coins minted by government

8. Duplicate all cards and provide a set of cards (card 1 only) to each group. Cards are to be discussed in relation to the list of qualifications previously discussed in class, and the two or three best and one worst candidates should be identified. Reasons should be provided for "best" and "worst."

9. Place a chart similar to figure 6.1 on the overhead or board. When all groups have made their decisions, have a representative from each group put the information into the chart. Provide answers to the question "Which card represents whom?"

| Group | Most Qualified Candidate | Least Qualified Candidate |
|-------|--------------------------|---------------------------|
| A     |                          |                           |
| B     |                          |                           |
| C     |                          |                           |

*Figure 6.1.*  *Comparison chart.*

10. Discuss: Why did the group make the selections they did? Why were some choices between groups similar and some not? Would you change your decisions now that you know whom the cards represented? If so, why? Should any factors have been considered other than those in your final list? If so, which factors and why? How did your group decide upon the two lists? Was group consensus necessary? If not, why not? How do people make their decisions about for whom to vote? Do your decisions reflect those of the people living in your community? Do your decisions reflect those of the rest of your class? What determines the qualities a person judges to be most important? How have the qualifications for a president probably changed over the years? Why?

11. Return to the KWL chart and have students provide the information needed to complete the L column of the chart. Point out (and/or delete) incorrect information from the K column that has now been corrected based on information provided in the L column.

**Extensions/Adaptations**

- Examine election requirements of other governments for various officials (Queen of England, prime minister of England, president of France) and replicate the procedure used for examining the office of the U.S. presidency.
- Limit information used on individual cards, or limit the number of cards provided to student groups (depending on grade level).
- Identify and execute a plan for determining the most desirable qualities in a presidential candidate in your neighborhood or school.
- Develop attribute cards for more recent presidential candidates or for a select number of historical presidents.
- Develop attribute cards for local officials, school officials, or class officers. Discuss how and if the qualities desirable in a president or other upper-level governmental officials are also appropriate at a more local level.

## Recommended Children's Books

Arnold, Emily. (1998). *The Ballot Box Battle*. Dragonfly Books.

Bartlett, Craig. (2000). *Arnold For President*. Simon Spotlight.

Brown, Marc. (1992). *Arthur Meets the President*. Little, Brown and Company.

Christelow, Eileen. (2004). *Vote!* Houghton Mifflin.

Granfield, Linda. (2003). *America Votes: How Our President is Elected*. Kids Can Press Ltd.

Harvey, Miles. (1996). *Presidential Elections*. Children's Press.

Sachar, Louis. (1999). *Class President*. Random House.

St. George, Judith. (2000). *So You Want to Be President?* Philomel.

Sisulu, Elinor Batezat. *The Day GoGo Went to Vote*. Little, Brown and Company.

Steir, Catherine. (1999). *If I Were President*. Albert Whitman and Company.

## Technology Resources

www.potus.com: Personal and political information on all of the U.S. presidents; also includes links to associated sites on the first ladies and other governmental officials.

www.send4fun.com/presidentdance.htm: Illustrations of the presidents dancing, singing, and telling about their contribution to history.

www.presidentsusa.net/pictures.html: Photographs or portraits of all the presidents.

## DOING, THINKING, FEELING, BEHAVING—AND CONSEQUENCES

Students will create graphic organizers that present alternative solutions to the problems of individuals and groups presented in *Yertle the Turtle and Other Stories* by Dr. Seuss.

Duration: 1 or more class periods

Group Size: full class

Disciplines: language arts, history, values education

Skills: describing, generalizing, classifying, evaluating, analyzing

Key Vocabulary: thoughts, feelings, actions, reacting, consequences; unknown story vocabulary

Materials: *Yertle the Turtle*, writing/drawing materials, turtle pattern, dry-erase or water soluble marker

## Procedure

1. Prior to reading the story, make multiple copies of a basic turtle pattern in four colors.
2. On four patterns (one of each color) write the following words: Action, Thoughts, Feelings, Consequences. Post these on wall or chart paper in one row. Laminate multiple copies of the turtles in various colors.
3. Read *Yertle the Turtle* to the class.
4. Model the following procedure to class:
   a. With students, select one example of a character's action in the story (e.g., Yertle surveyed his kingdom). Write action on a turtle pattern and discuss why this is an action. Place the turtle under appropriate column on wall.
   b. With students, select an example of a thought that the previous character experienced during the action (e.g., My kingdom is too small. I can't see enough). Write the action on the turtle template and discuss. Place it under the appropriate column.
   c. Together discuss how Yertle may be feeling as he thinks about the small kingdom (e.g., angry, frustrated). Write the "feeling description" on the turtle template and place it under the correct column.
   d. Discuss what Yertle decides to do because of his feelings (e.g., orders all of the turtles to make a stack so he can climb up and see a great distance). Write on the turtle template and place it under the correct column.
   e. Discuss what happens as a result of this action (e.g., The stack falls and Yertle gets stuck in the mud).
5. Repeat with the other characters in the story.
6. Repeat with the same characters and have students suggest alternatives such as the following:

Action: Yertle surveys his kingdom.
Thought: He is ruler of all he can see.
Feeling: Yertle is happy.
Reaction: A holiday is declared.
Consequence: Everyone has a good time.

7. Repeat, having the students apply this to events in the classroom as well as to other story characters. Discuss the differences that attitude and actions can make in the various situations.

## Extensions/Adaptations

- Create a graphic organizer with the book title in the center of the identified space and the four actions surrounding the outer edges of the image.
- Prewrite specific actions, thoughts, feelings, reactions, and consequences on turtle patterns and have students place in appropriate columns as the class discusses each.
- Use the above items (prewritten) as a folder game for individuals.
- Discuss why the turtles did as Yertle told them to do. What would have happened had they not obeyed him?

## Recommended Children's Books

Carlson, N. (1992). *Arnie and the Stolen Markers*. Penguin Group.
Gackenbach, D. (1989). *Hattie Rabbit*. Harper Collins.
Kirk, D. (1994). *Miss Spider's Tea Party*. Scholastic Press/Callaway.
Milne, A. A. (1999). *Winnie the Pooh and Some Bees*. Penguin Putnam Books.
Muth, J. (2002). *The Three Questions*. Scholastic Press.
Seuss, Dr. (1949). *Bartholomew and the Oobleck*. Random House.
Seuss, Dr. *Gertrude McFuzz*. Random House.
Seuss, Dr. (1991). *Six by Seuss*. Random House.
Seuss, Dr. (1990). *The 500 Hats of Bartholomew Huggins*. Random House.
Seuss, Dr. (1998). *The Big Brag*. Random House.
Seuss, Dr. (1971). *The Lorax*. Random House.
Seuss, Dr. (1958). *Yertle the Turtle and Other Stories*. Random House.

## Technology Resources

www.naspcenter.org/teachers/gc_stopthink.html: Information on teaching children interpersonal and conflict-resolution skills.
homepages.wmich.edu/~a3bailey/Building%20Blocks_files/page0002.htm: Information on self-management and choices.
www.scholastic.com/clifford/parentsteachers/teachers/lessonplans/truthful.htm: Lesson on following the golden rule using the *Clifford the Big Red Dog* books.

## PERSONAL RIGHTS AND RESPONSIBILITIES

By discussing the concept of responsibility and generating a classroom list of responsibilities to add to a Bill of Rights, students will gain an introductory understanding of the role of individual responsibility.

Duration: 2–3 class periods
Group Size: whole class and pairs
Disciplines: history, geography, language arts, fine arts
Skills: describing, interpreting, deducing, generalizing, analyzing, inferring
Key Vocabulary: citizen, citizenship, rights, responsibility, liberty, Bill of Rights
Materials: drawing paper, markers or crayons, world map

**Procedure**

1. Read *We the People* and *We the Kids* and discuss student observations on the illustrations.
2. Discuss citizenship (member of a community or group of people) and the rights and responsibilities that accompany being a citizen of a particular group (classroom, neighborhood, city, country). Discuss illustrations from the book that emphasized the rights and responsibilities of people. Focus on responsibility to include being able to take care of oneself, respecting the rights of others, and obeying rules and laws. Focus on rights to include the concept of liberty.
3. Read *Yertle the Turtle* and discuss the concept of rights. Have pairs of students generate a list of rights for the classroom.
4. Read *Horton Hatches the Egg* and discuss the concept of responsibility. Have pairs generate a list of responsibilities for the classroom.
5. As a class, discuss all lists and generate a master list for the classroom bill of rights.
6. Create with student assistance a T-chart that distinguishes between specific rights and responsibilities (freedom of speech, going where one wants to, choosing where to live, obeying traffic laws, using language appropriately, doing a job well, etc.)

## Extensions/Adaptations

- Give students opportunities to play board games in small groups. Discuss the rights and responsibilities needed by individuals to make the game a pleasant experience.
- Have students research local and national figures who exemplify looking out for the rights of others and who take responsibility for their actions.
- Focus on various patriotic symbols and celebrations and discuss their links with rights and responsibilities of citizens.

## Recommended Children's Books

Catrow, David. (2002). *We the Kids*. Scholastic.
Hamilton, John. (2004). *Bill of Rights*. ABDO Publishing.
Santos, Robin. (2003). *Citizenship*. Raintree Publishing.
Seuss, Dr. (1966). *Horton Hatches the Egg*. Random House
Seuss, Dr. (1958). *Yertle the Turtle and Other Stories*. Random House.
Spier, Peter. (1987). *We the People*. Doubleday.
Stadler, Alexander. (2003). *Beverly Billingsly Takes a Bow*. Harcourt Brace and Company.

## Technology Resources

www.billofrights.com/: Historical information, Amendments 1 through 10 of the Constitution, and many related links.
www.hrweb.org/: Information answering questions related to such questions as, What are human rights? How do we protect human rights? What are some human-rights resources? and What are the legal and political documents available related to human rights?
k-6educators.about.com/od/classroommanagement/a/Classroom_jobs.htm: Ways to teach responsibility through a variety of classroom jobs.

# CHAPTER 7

# Production, Distribution, and Consumption

Happiness is not in the mere possession of money; it lies in the joy of achievement, in the thrill of creative effort.

— Franklin D. Roosevelt

Never spend your money before you have it.

— Thomas Jefferson

Production, distribution, and consumption concepts demand use of reasoning processes by which students learn to understand and work with the idea of choice and consequences. Specifically, there are no costless decisions. Individuals must choose what will be given up (and what it will cost) as well as the resulting consequence—what will be gained once a choice is made. To become economically literate, students must develop the ability to effectively function in a global economy in relation to needs and wants, distribution, exchange, consumption of goods and services, and the use of limited resources to fulfill seemingly unlimited wants and needs. Unless students have background knowledge about the world and how it functions in relation to economics, and unless they have the skills necessary to make, save, and invest money, they will be unable to make good, informed choices and function effectively in a personal, local, or global economy. Activities that promote an appreciation of how individuals, groups, and cultures allocate and use resources in various ways provide opportunities for identifying and understanding alternatives, accepting consequences, recognizing that one can't have everything one might want, and accepting the choices and decisions of others. Effective activities incorporate the use of specific terminology such as resources, money, allocation, incentives, gain, profit, market economy, government policies, benefits, employment, institutions, goods, services, and budget to help prepare students with lifelong strategies for living in society.

## MOOSE, MUFFINS, AND MONEY

Using manipulatives that represent the goods and services found in *If You Give a Moose a Muffin*, students will differentiate between goods and services

> Duration: 1–2 class periods
> Group Size: whole class
> Disciplines: economics, language arts
> Skills: classification, cause and effect
> Key Vocabulary: goods, services, cause, effect, wants, needs
> Materials: markers, crayons, pencils, paper, magazines, glue or rubber cement, 3 × 5 index cards, *If You Give a Moose a Muffin* by Laura Joffee Numeroff, flannel board with two headings: goods and services.

### Procedure

1. Ask students if they have ever heard statements such as "If you finish your supper, you may have dessert"; "If you finish your homework, you may watch television"; or "If you stop talking, you may go out to play."
2. Explain that the first part of the sentence ("If you . . .") indicates cause—tells something that might happen. Explain that the second part of the sentence tells what might happen because of the first part of the sentence (the effect).
3. Have students brainstorm other cause-and-effect sentences. Discuss the cause and effect of each.
4. Read the book title, *If You Give a Moose a Muffin*, to the class. Have students predict the effect of the thought described in the sentence.
5. Explain that in this story the moose has many things he wants. These things the moose wants are goods and services.

6. Discuss goods (things that can be touched and used) and services (things that someone does for you or that you can do for someone else). Have students provide examples of each. Categorize the responses on a chart for everyone to view:

| Goods | Services |
|-------|----------|
| cookies | bakery |
| cars | automobile factory |

7. Tell students to listen, as the story is read, for items the moose wants or acts in which the moose is involved and to decide if each is a good or a service.
8. After the story is read, have students locate examples in magazines of the items and acts from the story. Each student cuts out and attaches an example to an index card. Glue a small piece of flannel to the back of each card. Cards are placed in a prepared box labeled goods and services.
9. Individual students select cards from the box. Have the group decide under which heading on the flannel board the card should be placed. Discuss why each belongs where it does. Continue until all have been placed on the flannel board.
10. Review: What are goods? What are services? Discuss: How are goods and services similar? How are goods and services different? What are some goods or services you would like to have? If you were _____ (identify a famous person), what types of goods and services do you think you might want that are different from those you want now?

**Extensions/Adaptations**

- Class members write a cause-and-effect story of their choosing, with each person contributing in a round-robin format: "If you give a _____ a _____, then he/she/it will want a _____." The next person adds to this, then the next, until all students have contributed.
- Create illustrations to accompany the above contributions. Attach these to a bulletin board, thereby creating a classroom storyboard.
- Apply cause-and-effect and goods-and-services concepts to elements in history, such as the following: "What might Eli Whitney

have wanted for his cotton? Once he got the cotton gin, then what might he have wanted?"

- Have students use paper, markers, and crayons to develop representations of items for a bulletin board called "Goods and Services."
- Develop mini-stories to share with students. Underline specific items in the story and have students identify each as a good or a service, such as the following:
  - If you give a toad a tickle, he will probably start to laugh.
  - He may laugh so hard he gets the hiccups.
  - If he gets the hiccups, he may want a glass of water.
  - If you give him a glass of water, he may spill it.
  - If he spills it, he may want a mop to clean up the spill.

### Recommended Children's Books

Axelrod, Amy. (1997). *Pigs Will Be Pigs: Fun with Math and Money*. Aladdin Paperbacks.

Numeroff, Laura Joffee. (1985). *If You Give a Mouse a Cookie*. Harper Collins.

Numeroff, Laura Joffee. (1998). *If You Give a Pig a Pancake*. Harper Collins.

Numeroff, Laura Joffee. (2000). *If You Take a Mouse to the Movies*. Harper Collins.

Wilson, Antoine. (2000). *Young Zillionaires Guide to Distributing Goods and Services*. Rosen Publishing Group.

### Technology Resources

www.nyapplecountry.com/nysapplemuffin.htm: The official New York state apple muffin recipe and other apple recipes.

www.city.toronto.on.ca/moose/moose_kids.htm: A fun fashion site for moose.

www.kidsturncentral.com/links/elkmooselinks.htm: Links to "moose" sites.

### Goods and Services Flannel Board Pieces

Cut out and duplicate the square flannel board pieces. Attach one piece of velcro or flannel to the back of each for use on a flannel board.

## SELLING HATS

Students will discuss various purposes of hats and will design, advertise, and market their hat creations.

Duration: 1–2 class periods
Group Size: individuals, pairs, or groups of three
Disciplines: economics, history, language arts, mathematics
Skills: communication
Key Vocabulary: bias, propaganda, marketing, advertising, exchange rates
Materials: markers, pencils, pens, paper of different sizes and colors, *Caps For Sale* by E. Slobodkina.

## Procedure

1. Read *Caps for Sale* with the class. Discuss how hats were sold in *Caps for Sale* and how caps and hats are sold today. Discuss hats and caps as related to cultural and regional differences: In which cultures is it more prevalent for people to wear hats? Why is this a common practice in these cultures? In the United States, why are men asked to take off their hats at certain times? What specific times are men asked to remove their hats? Do you feel this is necessary, or is it a habit? Why?
2. Show pictures of several types of hats. Discuss what purpose certain hats serve: bowlers, ten-gallon hat, sombrero, ski mask, and so on?
3. Discuss such components of an advertisement as jingles, bias, and propaganda techniques. By entering "hats" into most Internet search engines, students can locate dozens of hat-related sites in many locations around the world.
4. Have students create their own caps or hats and market them through advertisements. Determine the price at which each hat will be sold. Use factors such as the time to make each hat, the hourly wage for a hat maker, the cost of the materials, and the profit desired to help determine the price.
5. Give students word problems to solve that require them to use information from the sites found above: What is the difference

between the U.S. price and the Australian price of one Acoolah hat? How much money could you save per hat if you bought two Acoolah hats instead of only one? www.xe.net/currency/.

6. Have students use websites to develop their own word problems. Students exchange problems and locate answers.

7. Introduce the concepts of labor, capital, private ownership, profits, management, goods and services, and favorable conditions. Have students create a hat business or manufacturing plant.

8. Have students borrow money from a "bank" to establish their business. How much would be borrowed and at what percent interest? How much must each hat sell for in order to cover the overhead, bills, and pay back the loan to the bank? When will the bank be repaid in full?


### Recommended Children's Books

Bawden, Juliet. (1994). *The Hat Book*. Lark Books.
Karon, Jan. (1998). *Miss Fannie's Hat*. Augsburg Fortress Publishers.
Krisher, Trudy. (1992). *Kathy's Hats: A Story of Hope*. Concept Books.
Nodset, Joan L. (1988). *Who Took the Farmer's Hat?* Harper Trophy.
Reynolds, Helen. (2003). *Hats and Hairstyles*. Raintree Publishing.
Reynolds, William. (1995). *The Cowboy Hat Book*. Gibbs Smith Publisher.
Seuss, Dr. (1989). *The 500 Hats of Bartholomew Cubbins*. Random House.
Shultz, Charles. (2000). *Caps Don't Win Ballgames, Marcie*. Harper Collins.
Steig, William. (2003). *When Everybody Wore a Hat*. Harper Collins.


### Technology Resources

www.yosemite.net/bwear/: Kuffis, handmade caps from authentic African fabrics imported from Ghana.
www.millerhats.com: Australian outback hats.
www.deelightful.com/: Delightful Lids: variety of Canadian hats, jester hats, hoho hats, touques, and the like.


## STOP THE SPIES

As students "travel" around the world in search of world-renowned spies, they will determine costs of items and calculate exchange rates.

Duration: 1–2 class periods
Group Size: pairs or small groups of 3–4
Disciplines: economics, geography, mathematics
Skills: communicating, interpreting, analyzing, deducing, inferring, evaluating
Key Vocabulary: currency exchange
Materials: introductory information, clue cards, Web addresses for currency, exchange rates, pencils, paper, world maps, calculator (1 per group), *Eyewitness: Money* by Joe Cribb. (See sections at the end of this actitity for some of this material.)

**Procedure**

Prior to the activity, reproduce the clues on index cards to be used as clue cards for the groups or hand out a one-page sheet with clues to each group.

*Part 1*

1. Review the world map locating continents, major countries, and major bodies of water.
2. Discuss currency exchange rates (and how they change) and the relationship between the U.S. dollar and various other types of money. Discuss how the Euro can be used in many countries but how some countries still retain the currency used prior to the Euro as well. Provide students with Web addresses where current exchange rates can be located.
3. Present the introductory story information to the students. As a group, discuss the first clue: The thieves have been spotted eating fish and chips at a café in Carnarvon just outside the castle gates. Apparently they rented a flat for 1,000 while they were in this location. Identify key words and places in the clue that will help students locate the country.
4. Identify (with the students) (1) the country, (2) the type of money, and (3) the exchange rate. Model the way to calculate the dollar equivalent for the price using the current exchange rate.

*Part 2*

1. Distribute clue cards, maps, and calculators to groups.
2. Identify the roles for each person in each group (combine jobs as necessary):

   clue reader—reads each clue aloud to the group

   country marker—flags/marks the country once the group has identified the location

   bookkeeper—determines exchange-rate equivalents using the calculator

   recorder—keeps record of the country, the type of money, and the exchange equivalent for the group

   money identifier—uses resource books to identify the type of money used by the country identified

   rate exchange locator/researcher—locates current exchange rates for use by the bookkeeper
3. Have students begin working on the clues, modeling after the process used for the clue in part 1. Encourage discussion among the members of each pair or group as they begin to read clues and identify countries. It is no one particular person's job to find the countries—it should be a group effort. Have students change jobs after every two cards so that all can experience the various aspects of the activity.
4. Discuss the results from each group and review/investigate any items where answers differ among groups. Have students identify key words from the clues that helped locate the countries. Discuss differences among exchange rates.

**Extensions/Adaptations**

- Review fall 2000 news reports on Tyson espionage and stealing of industrial secrets regarding the Tyson chicken feed formula.
- Have students develop clue cards for other locations where the spies of the Farm Animal Feed Formula Group have been sighted.
- Rearrange the clue cards so that teams of students can compete against one another. Keep track of their progress on a class world map.

## Recommended Children's Books

Adshead, Paul. (1996). *Around the World with Phineas Frog: A Geographic Puzzle*. Child's Play International.

Cribb, Joe. (2000). *Eyewitness: Money*. D. K. Publishing.

Evans, Douglas. (2004). *MVP*. Front Street Incorporated.

Fitzhugh, Louise. (2001). *Harriet the Spy*. Yearling Books.

Godfrey, Neal. (1998). *The Ultimate Kids' Money Book*. Simon and Schuster Books for Young Readers.

Mason, Antony. (1995). *Around the Word in 80 Pages: An Adventurous Picture Atlas of the World*. Copper Beech Books.

Poole, Hazel (ed.). (2000). *Spies and Detectives*. Penguin Books.

Scillan, Devin. (2003). *P is for Passport: A World Alphabet*. Sleeping Bear Press.

## Technology Resources

www.xe.net/currency/: Converts major world currencies.

www.womenswire.com/bloomberg/currency.html: Currency converter calculator for over 200 foreign currencies.

www.oanda.com/cgi-bin/ncc: Currency converter for over 164 world currencies.

## Introduction Information for "Stop the Spies"

You have been contacted by a top-secret agency within your country to help track down a group of international spies. These spies, an organization known as the Farm Animal Feed Formula Group (FFFG), work around the world stealing secrets from agricultural companies, particularly those involved in the production of poultry products. The FFFG infiltrates a company in one area of the world, gains the trust of its employees, steals top-secret information, and then relocates to sell the information to the highest bidder. Sometimes, when it appears as though law enforcement officials are about to catch up with them, members of the FFFG will lay low for a while until it seems safe to invade another company.

The task your team has been given is to track the spies through their credit card trail. You will be provided information about the countries where the FFFG have been located and the amount they charged on a stolen credit card. When you are able to identify the country, find out what monetary unit is used by the country, check the exchange rate, and calculate how much money has been spent at that location. Keep track of your information on a chart (similar to the following example). If you figure out each country, monetary unit, and have calculated the exchange rates correctly, you will receive an award for your assistance in locating and capturing the FFFG. Good Luck!

| Clue Number | Country | Monetary Unit | Exchange Rate | Amount Spent |
|---|---|---|---|---|
| 1 | Wales | pound | | |
| 9 | Italy | lire | | $2,000 |

**Clue Cards**

1. The thieves have been spotted eating fish and chips at a café in Carnarvon just outside the castle gates. Apparently they rented a flat for 1,000 while they were in this location.
2. FFFG members crossed the channel on the ferry spending approximately 25 during the trip.
3. The rental car the group needed to get to Lyon cost $300 American. How much in the local currency?
4. The group was out of sight for a few days, but they resurfaced after paying 8,000 for warm clothing in Goteborg.
5. For $36,000 American, the spies bought a new M class in which to travel down the Autobahn. How much did they pay the locals?
6. The FFFG members stayed out of sight until they were spotted singing Waltzing Matilda in the outback with a large amount of camping equipment that cost 65,000.
7. A lacrosse match in Montreal was the next place the FFFG members were spotted. They spent 450 on refreshments and tickets and then stole transportation to their next destination.
8. After playing mah-jongg in Xi'an and losing 5,400, the spies traveled west.
9. They spent $2,000 American in Venice because of wrecking a gondola.

10. The FFFG was spotted viewing the site of the very first Olympics. They spent 600 on souvenirs.
11. In Kuala Lumpur the FFFG spent $2,000 American to watch the Formula I Grand Prix Race. How much in the local currency?
12. The group purchased a sailboat for 450,000 DM in Dusseldorf. How much American money did they spend?
13. After participating in the Running of the Bulls, group members spent about $2,000 American in the hospital emergency room.
14. The hotel bill for a week in Cozumel was $3,200 American. How much did they spend in local currency?
15. A visit to Ocho Rios cost the group $4,600 American. How much did they spend in local currency?
16. At the GUM department store in Moscow, the members spent 12,000. How much in American currency?

**Country Answer Key**

| | |
|---|---|
| 1. Wales | 9. Italy |
| 2. English Channel | 10. Greece |
| 3. France | 11. Malaysia |
| 4. Sweden | 12. Germany |
| 5. Germany | 13. Spain |
| 6. Australia | 14. Mexico |
| 7. Canada | 15. Jamaica |
| 8. China | 16. Russia |

## PURCHASING POWER

Students will become familiar with the concepts of wants and needs while developing commercial advertisements, purchasing items, and maintaining a bank balance.

Duration: 2–3 class periods
Group Size: student pairs or entire class
Disciplines: economics, math, language arts, fine arts
Skills: application, prediction, inference, synthesis, communication, problem solving, decision making

Key Vocabulary: wants, needs, grocery, supermarket, advertise, economics

Materials: newspaper grocery-store advertisements, writing materials, chart paper, crayons, play money (for amount, see part 2, item 1), *The Witches' Supermarket* by S. Meddaugh.

**Procedure**

*Part 1*

1. Discuss key vocabulary. Allow students to provide examples and nonexamples of wants and needs. Read *The Witches' Supermarket* aloud to class.

2. Have students brainstorm a list of items found in the witches' supermarket and write a list on the board or overhead. Prompt students to add items to the list that were not in the story but that might be found in such a store.

3. Divide the class into student pairs and have each pair examine several grocery store advertisements from the newspaper. Have each pair share with the class the information they find in the advertisements (cost, pictures, descriptions, etc.) Student pairs will select an item they might find in a witches' supermarket for which they will create a one-page newspaper advertisement using actual advertisements as models. These ads must include an appropriate price, written description, and illustrations.

4. Within the room, the teacher should have two columns of chart paper, one identifying wants and the other needs. Student pairs will share their advertisements, discussing with the class whether the items should be considered a want or a need. (Viewpoints will vary; teachers should accept all, provided the students can establish a rationale). Hang individual advertisements in the correct column on the chart paper. Discuss: What is a want? What is a need? Why might some people think they need something while others might think the same item is a want? If a large number of people decide they are going to buy something, what do you think

it will do to the price of the item? Why? If no one wants to buy an item, what do you think it will do to the price of the item? Why? Brainstorm some specific items for which this is evidenced (e.g., gasoline, land, gold, etc.).

5. Have students share examples of items in their lives that could be considered wants and/or needs. Write a list of these items on the board or overhead. Have students estimate prices for these items. (Use catalogs and newspaper advertisements if guidance is needed). Discuss: What makes these items different from the items in the witches' supermarket? If you had some money, which would you rather buy, one of the items from the witches' supermarket or one of the items that we just listed? Why?

## Part 2

1. Distribute play money to students (amount is determined by price of most expensive item in part 1). Review money amounts if necessary. Have students count the money they have been given. Discuss that money can be used to purchase one expensive item or several inexpensive items.

2. Select an item from the student-created advertisements. Have students identify the amount of money they would need to buy the item. Have students count out the correct number of coins needed to purchase the item. Repeat this process for several items.

3. Tell students they may now decide on which items they may spend their money. Students can work independently or in pairs to determine which items they want or need. Each student should create a table identifying the item(s) bought, price paid, and balance left. Be sure to have students indicate their starting balance first in the balance column before purchasing an item.

4. Discuss: Which items did you buy? Why did you choose these items? Were these items wants or needs? Did you choose to spend your money all on one item or on several items? Why did you make this choice? Did you have any money left over? If so, how much? What are some things you could do with this leftover money? How could you add to this leftover money so that you could purchase

more items? Should you purchase items that you want when there are items that you need? Why or why not? What are some things you should consider when planning on spending money?

## Extensions/Adaptations

- Focus on bias and propaganda techniques used in advertising.
- Share grocery advertisements with the entire class and discuss advertising information.
- Have students draw and cut out pictures to put on a class advertisement.
- Students will dictate information to the teacher for the advertisement (cost, description).
- For any of the children's books listed below, change items for which students initially create advertisements to parallel book contents.

## Recommended Children's Books

Axelrod, Amy. (1999). *Pigs Go to Market: Fun with Math and Shopping*. Aladdin Paperbacks.
Bendick, Jeanne. (1997). *Markets: From Barter to Bar Codes*. Franklin Watts.
McMillan, B. (1996). *Jelly Beans for Sale*. Scholastic.
Rocklin, JoAnne. (1999). *The Case of the Shrunken Allowance*. Scholastic.
Shea, Kitty. (2004). *Out and About at the Supermarket*. Picture Window Books.
Slobodkina, E. (1988). *Caps for Sale*. Harper Collins Juvenile Books.
Vaughan, M. (1999). *Lemonade Stand*. Grossett and Dunlap.
Viorst, J. (1999). *Alexander Who Used to Be Rich Last Sunday*. EconoClad Books.

## Technology Resources

historymatters/gmu.mse/Ads/online.html: A collection of websites about the history of advertising.
www.kidsbank.com: Teaches the principles of banking at the elementary level.
Advertising.harpweek.com/: The history of advertising in the nineteenth century.

## A MONEY STORY

Using an equivalency table, students will construct, illustrate, and describe money equivalencies using pennies, nickels, dimes, and quarters to equal one dollar.

Duration: 1–3 class periods
Group Size: individually or small groups
Disciplines: history, mathematics, language arts, economics
Skills: categorizing, measuring, comparing, predicting
Key Vocabulary: penny, nickel, dime, quarter, dollar, equivalent
Materials: money chart (either duplicated for each group or student or enlarged for use with entire class), money stories, money pictures (duplicated for individuals or groups), writing materials, *Alexander Who Used to Be Rich Last Sunday* by Judith Viorst.

### Procedure

1. Read *Alexander Who Used to be Rich Last Sunday* with class. Discuss the types of information Alexander needed to know in order to spend his money (what each piece of money is worth, physical money characteristics).

2. Discuss the money pictures. Have students separate and classify picture money into categories: brown coin, small silver coin, large silver coin, rectangular money, other coins. Have students identify particular items related to each piece: Select the brown coin. Who is the picture on the brown coin? (Lincoln) Select the largest silver coin. What is the word on the bottom of the back of the coin? (Quarter) How much is a quarter worth? (Twenty-five cents) Continue. After discussing each coin using several questions, have students use a money-comparison chart (such as the one shown in figure 7.1) as guided practice, either in groups, as individuals, or on the overhead projector with the entire class. Review the correct information.

3. Have students place all the money pictures in front of them. Have students select and hold up the following: one piece of money that is equivalent to 10 pennies, two pieces of money that are equivalent

| Ways of Writing | Heads | Tails | Equivalents |
|---|---|---|---|
| Penny | | | |
| Nickel | | | |
| Dime | | | |
| Quarter | | | |

**Figure 7.1.** *Money comparison chart.*

to 10 pennies, one piece of money that is equivalent to one dollar, four pieces of money that are equivalent to one dollar, and one piece of money that is equivalent to twenty-five cents.

4. Have students place the money on the left side of their desks. Move the following to the center of the desk: the amount of pennies you would need to be the equivalent of one nickel, the amount of nickels you would need to be the equivalent of one quarter, the amount of quarters you would need to be the equivalent of one dollar, the minimum combination of coins you would need to be the equivalent of one quarter (you must use at least two types of coins), the coins you would need to be the equivalent of one dollar (you must use at least two types of coins), and the coins you would need to be the equivalent of one dime (you must use at least two types of coins).

5. Put the first money story on the overhead. Have students identify the coins needed to purchase an item in the money story. Have students identify one alternate set of coins equal to the amount of money needed to purchase the item. Students should use the money pictures on their desks to accomplish each task. The teacher should walk around the room to monitor student responses. Repeat this procedure for each additional money story.

**Extensions/Adaptations**

- Have students construct their own (or group) money stories. Save these stories for a couple of days and then have the students respond to the stories as they did in the instructions above.
- Identify additional equivalencies that require more detailed thinking.
- Use types of money from foreign countries (e.g., yen, mark, pound, lire, Euro).
- Identify equivalencies for greater amounts of money, such as four columns labeled five dollar bill, ten dollar bill, twenty dollar bill, fifty dollar bill. Students develop equivalencies for each (e.g., ten dollars equals two five dollar bills or ten one dollar bills or one five dollar bill and five one dollar bills). Compare the Euro with the American dollar.
- Use the classified sections of foreign newspapers (England or Australia) with students. Have them determine equivalence between the cost of items in these places with the cost in the United States.

**Recommended Children's Books**

Kummer, Patricia K. (2004). *Currency*. Scholastic.
Lanczak, Rozanne. (2003). *Learning about Coins*. Gareth Stevens Audio.
Riley, Kathryn. (1999). *The Big Sale*. Millbrook Press Tradebooks.
Rocklin, Joanne. (1995). *How Much is That Guinea Pig in the Window?* Scholastic.
Schwartz, David. (1993). *How Much is a Million?* Mulberry Books.
Schwartz, David. (1994). *If You Made a Million*. Mulberry Books.
Viorst, J. (1999). *Alexander Who Used to Be Rich Last Sunday*. EconoClad Books.
Young, Robert. (1998). *Money (Household History)*. Carolrhoda Books.

**Technology Resources**

Oanda.com/convert/classic: Currency conversion site.
www.pbs.org/newshour/on2/money/history.html: A story about the history of money from prehistory through today.
www.factmonster.com/ipka/A0774856.html: The history of money (1690 to present) for the United States.

**Money Stories**

1. Each piece of candy costs one penny. How many pennies do you need to buy 10 pieces of candy?

2. You think 100 pennies are too many to carry around in your pocket or purse. What coins, equivalent in value, could you carry that would not take up so much room?

3. You want to spend your 25 cents on a present for a friend. What coins could you use to buy the present?

4. You have three dimes and two nickels. How much money do you have? What other coins could you have that would equal the same amount of money?

5. What should Alexander have done in each situation when he traded money?

# CHAPTER 8

# Science, Technology, and Society

Society lives by faith and develops by science.

—Henri Frederic Amiel

It has often been stated that the only constant in society is change. Within world societies, the constant advances made in technology and the sciences continue to foster changes in society and have resulted in encouraging people in contemporary society to live in an immediate "need to know" way of thinking. Ideas related to science, technology, and society often generate questions for students. What would life be like today if certain things didn't exist? What can we learn about the past using today's technologies? What can we predict about the future? How can we use science and technology to help us create a better society? Do scientific and technological advances really make life better, or do they only make life different? How will people and their belief systems change as science and technology promote more changes in society?

To change and keep up with the changing times, students must develop skills that promote lifelong learning through refined abilities to make informed decisions, solve problems, and engage in inquiry. Additionally, they must participate in experiences that promote self-direction and self-regulation. In order to acquire these skills and personal abilities, students must be involved in practices that help them define science and technology. They must also learn about how society influences science and technology as well as how science and technology influence society. Knowledge related to science, technology, and society is primarily acquired through the areas of the natural sciences, physical sciences, social sciences, humanities, and mathematics.

## CRIME SOLVING

Students will examine how science and technology assist in solving the breaking of society's laws.

Duration: 1–2 class sessions
Group Size: groups of 4–5
Disciplines: history, sociology, fine arts, language arts, math, science
Skills: classifying, categorizing, analyzing, record keeping, evaluating, interpreting, describing
Key Vocabulary: investigate, investigation, fingerprinting, investigators, FBI, culprit, latent print, plastic print, forensic scientist
Materials: pencils, paper, fingerprinting worksheet (see the section at the end of this activity), fingerprinting background, tape, overhead projector, transparencies, empty glass jar

**Procedure**

1. Have students brainstorm about when they have seen fingerprints. On what kinds of surfaces do fingerprints show up? How do they think we can use fingerprints? Discuss information on the background of fingerprinting.
2. Divide class into groups. Provide each group with a fingerprinting worksheet so they can each record the fingerprints of each student in their group. To make fingerprints, each student should do the following:
   a. Rub an area on a piece of paper with a pencil (darkly).
   b. Rub a finger over the pencil lead (graphite) on the paper.
   c. Apply a small piece of clear tape to the finger, lift from finger, and place the tape in the appropriate box on the fingerprinting worksheet.
   d. Repeat for each finger on each hand.

3. Place tape pieces of various students' fingerprints on a transparency and show them to the entire class using the overhead projector. Compare and contrast the fingerprints using the three basic fingerprint types: plain arch, plain whorl, loop.

4. Before going to the next step, make a set of fingerprints (from several fingers of one person, either from the class or not) that can be put on an overhead projector. Then share the following story: "A couple of days ago, someone put sugar in the saltshaker in the teachers' workroom. Yesterday, someone put sugar in the saltshakers in the lunchroom, but luckily the lunchroom staff discovered it before we all went to lunch. This morning, the principal found a large jar like this one (show an empty jar) that contained traces of a granular white substance. The jar was found outside beside the trash cans. The substance in the jar was determined to be salt. Upon investigation, a set of fingerprints was found on the jar. Your job is to examine a copy of the fingerprints and decide if anyone in this class is the culprit in this crime." Then put the fingerprints on the overhead.

5. After allowing sufficient time to determine if any of the fingerprints are from a class member, discuss the problem-solving process that was involved as you examined the fingerprints. Construct a chart that outlines the problem-solving process as identified and used by the students.

**Extensions/Adaptations**

- Within their groups, have students create mystery stories that involve fingerprinting. The groups will exchange their stories and fingerprint worksheets and attempt to solve the mysteries.
- Additional ways to fingerprint:
  - Give each student a clean piece/section of glass. Have them rub a finger across the bridge of their nose and make a fingerprint on the glass. Sprinkle cocoa powder over the glass and carefully brush the powdered area with a fine paintbrush to remove excess powder and expose the print. (If dark glass or plastic is used, use talcum powder instead of cocoa.)

- Give each student a small piece of metal or plastic. Have them rub a finger across the bridge of their nose and make a fingerprint on the object. Place the object in a jar and place several drops of super glue in the jar (but be sure not to get any glue on the fingerprint). Close the lid of the jar and wait approximately 30 minutes. The print will appear to be white.
- Have students examine and compare shoe prints, lip prints, and handwriting as other ways of investigation.
- Scan fingerprints into a computer database to use in class when solving other crimes generated by the students.

## Recommended Children's Books

Conrad, Hy. (1998). *The Little Giant Book of Whodunits*. Sterling Publishing.
Dixon, Franklin. (1991). *The House on the Cliff*. Grosset & Donlap.
Jones, Charlotte, & Klein, David. (1997). *Fingerprints and Talking Bones: How Real Life Crimes are Solved*. Delacort Press.
Sharmat, Marjorie. (2002). *Nate the Great*. Delacorte.
Titos, Eve. (1989). *Basil of Beker Street*. Aladdin.
Wiese, Jim, & Shems, Ed. (1996). *Detective Science: 40 Crime-Solving, Case-Breaking, Crook-Catching Activities for Kids*. Wiley and Sons, Inc.

## Technology Resources

memory.loc.gov/learn/features/detect/mystery.html: A Library of Congress site allowing kids to become a historical detective.
www.worldartswest.org/plm/guide/activitypages/kidsroom/detective.shtml: An activity for students to role-play as folklore detectives.
www.media-awareness.ca/english/teachers/index.cfm: A source for teachers, with student activities that promote the investigation of television.

## Fingerprinting Worksheet

Construct a fingerprinting worksheet, like the one in figure 8.1, on an 8.5 × 11-inch sheet of paper. Leave enough room in each area for the student to imprint his or her fingerprint.

| Student 1 | Student 2 | Student 3 | Student 4 | Student 5 |
| --- | --- | --- | --- | --- |

right thumb

right index

right middle

right ring

right pinkie

left thumb

left index

left middle

left ring

left pinkie

**Figure 8.1.**   *Fingerprinting worksheet.*

## WHAT WOULD THE WORLD BE LIKE WITHOUT . . . ?

Students will compare technological advances of the historical world with the world in the present time.

Duration: 1 class session
Group Size: whole class
Disciplines: geography, history, sociology, anthropology, fine arts, language arts, math, science, health
Skills: classifying, categorizing, analyzing, record keeping, evaluating, interpreting, describing
Key Vocabulary: technological advances, component
Materials: writing and drawing materials, chart paper, newspapers

## Procedure

1. Have students brainstorm differences in society between the present time and 100 years ago, 50 years ago, 25 years ago, 10 years ago, and 5 years ago. List their ideas on chart paper.

2. Select one item (such as electricity). Divide class into small groups and have each develop a plan for one day: How would you get through the day without any electricity? Share information (including illustrations) with the class. Discuss implications for the family unit. At various times, discuss thought-provoking issues such as the following: What if computers and mobile phones didn't exist? How many electrical plugs do you have in your home? What is always plugged in? Why? If you had to give away one electrical thing that you use regularly, what would it be, and what could you use to replace it?

3. Select articles from the newspaper. In pairs, read the articles and identify items within them that relate to science or technology. Do all articles (sports, headlines, advertisements, etc.) include some components related to science and technology? What are they? If a scientific or technological component is not specifically stated, is it implied in any way? How? Why?

## Extensions/Adaptations

- Numbers in society: Explore the idea that everything is based on size (e.g., "Supersize it"). How do we use numbers (zip codes, area codes, ranking people, grades, etc.)?

- Trace the development of "new" inventions: computers, refrigeration, automobiles, telephones, and the like.

- Trace the development of music: reel-to-reel tapes, 8-tracks, cassette tapes, phonograph records, digitized CD, iPod. What are some advantages and disadvantages of each?

- Examine food inventions (pretzels, pizza, hot dogs, other snack foods). What would life be like today if they didn't exist?

- Compare and contrast different types of exercise equipment (treadmills, bicycles, weight machines) with ways people "kept in shape" before they existed.

## Recommended Children's Books

Bosveld, Jane, & O'Leary, Daniel. (1997). *While a Tree Was Growing*. Workman Publishing.
Brown, Marc. (1999). *Arthur's Computer Disaster*. Little, Brown and Company.
Dyson, Marianne. (2003). *Home on the Moon*. National Geographic Society.
Guthridge, Sue. (1986). *Thomas Edison: Young Inventor*. Aladdin.
Hammontree, Marie. (1986). *Albert Einstein: Young Thinker*. Aladdin.
Scrace, Carolyn, & Bennett, Paol. (1995). *What Was It Like Before Electricity?* Steck Vaughn.

## Technology Resources

www.eskimo.com/~billb/amasci.html: Amateur science site with links and activities for kids.
www.opticalres.com/kidoptx.html: Optics for children including how optics is a technological facet of society.
www.mtsociety.org/education/links.cfm: A site index for students concerning news on science and technology.

## GLITTERGERMS

Students will become aware of how infectious diseases can be transmitted.

Duration: 1 class session
Group Size: whole class
Disciplines: geography, history, anthropology, math, science
Skills: classifying, categorizing, analyzing, record keeping, evaluating, interpreting, describing
Key Vocabulary: infectious, transmit, communicable, noninfectious, noncommunicable
Materials: glitter, hand cream

### Procedure

1. Select three students to put hand lotion on their hands and then place glitter on their hands so that the glitter covers their hands (sticking to the hand lotion).

2. Students go around the room and shake one another's hands in greeting. Students greeted by the initial students can also greet one another with handshakes.
3. Discuss how the glitter transferred from person to person. Compare with infectious germs and diseases. Discuss how quickly the glitter transferred from person to person and the importance of washing hands.
4. Send students to wash hands with water only. (Glitter will not all wash off). Then wash with soap and water. Discuss the use of soap and washing hands as the biggest deterrent to the spread of germs.

### Extensions/Adaptations

- Identify each person with a number. As students shake hands with one another they keep track of the persons to whom they transmit the glitter. Tally and discuss multiple infections. Discuss and construct a diagram of the spread of germs that could occur between classrooms. Predict how the spreading of germs can occur geographically.
- Discuss noninfectious diseases (cancer, anemia, tetanus, environmental poisoning, etc.).
- Develop a Venn diagram that displays characteristics of infectious and noninfectious diseases.
- On a time line, identify the spread of germs throughout history (e.g., yellow fever, typhoid, etc.) and discuss why these types of germs are less likely to spread today.

### Recommended Children's Books

Day, N. (2001). *Malaria, West Nile and Other Mosquito Borne Diseases*. Enslow Publishers.

Friedlander, Mark. (2000). *Outbreak: Disease Detectives at Work*. Lerner Publishing.

Murphy, Jim. (2003). *American Plague: The True and Terrifying Story of the Yellow Fever Epidemic of 1793*. Clarion Books.

Wilson, Sarah. (1998). *Tommy Catches a Cold*. Simon & Schuster.

## Technology Resources

www.pkids.org/idw.htm: Information about disease and disease prevention.
serendip.brnmawr.edu/sci_edu/Waldron/infectious.html: Activity and information about how infectious diseases spread infectious agents.
www.chp.edu/greystone/infectious/pid.php: Ways to prevent the spread of infectious disease.


## INFORMATION RETRIEVAL CHARTS: SAMPLES OF ANCIENT CIVILIZATIONS, NATIVE AMERICAN POPULATIONS, AND SYSTEMS OF COMMUNICATION

Compilation of information on a particular topic in the form of an information retrieval chart allows students to easily collect data and compare and contrast information. See figure 8.2 for a sample chart.

Duration: ongoing
Group Size: small groups
Disciplines: geography, history, sociology, anthropology, fine arts
Skills: classifying, categorizing, analyzing, record keeping, evaluating, interpreting, describing
Key Vocabulary: specific according to topic of charts
Materials: sample retrieval charts, resource books on topic (minimum of 10 per topic), writing materials


## Procedure

*Part 1—Background on Retrieval Chart Construction*

1. Discuss with students the components needed for a chart to be effective (title, columns, rows, labeling of components, organization of components, source). Brainstorm reasons for using charts to compile information rather than writing a narrative or answering questions about the topic.
2. Construct two basic sample retrieval charts, one focusing on decoding information from a predesigned chart and one focusing on encoding information into chart form. Show the Sample Retrieval Chart 1 transparency. Read with students and together decode the

information to answer questions. Show a transparency with a blank retrieval chart. Allow students to provide the column and row headings as well as the information based on some aspect of the class familiar to everyone or with information easy to obtain (e.g., information about students in the class, types of food served for lunch each day that week, etc.)

3. Brainstorm with students to develop questions about information on the retrieval chart. Discuss how the chart must be used to be able to effectively read and interpret the information and answer questions. (Focus on matching information between columns and rows.)

*Part 2*

1. Divide the class into small groups of four to five. Allow each group to pick a topic (group) by drawing from the "hat" (e.g., Native American populations could include Northeast, Southwest, or Eastern, or specific tribes such as Seminole, Catawba, Cherokee, Navajo, Pawnee, or Miami). Have students identify in each group the member who is responsible for collecting information on a particular aspect of the culture they will be studying. For example, information on Native Americans of the plains could focus on location, climate, dwelling type, materials used in construction, and an important fact unique to the group being studied. (For a group of four students, each can focus on one of the first four rows, as indicated below. The final "fact" row can be one to which each person in the group must contribute.)

2. Using resource books, students collect information related to their topic and draw (create, copy, or duplicate) the appropriate illustration to be placed in each row. Upon completion of the retrieval-chart rows for their topic, each group identifies four to five questions they will ask to the rest of the class, using the retrieval chart as the source of information. For example:

Location: U.S. map outline with area colored

Climate: graph comparing summer and winter temperatures

Dwelling type: drawing of tepee

Materials used in construction: buffalo hides and poles

Important fact: portable villages were built so the Indians could follow buffalo herds

## Extensions/Adaptations

Retrieval charts can be constructed with the entire class providing information to the teacher and with the teacher putting information on a chart located in the room. Two additional retrieval charts are located at the end of this section.

Information is provided by students on index cards, and the index cards are attached with Velcro or other material to the chart.

Information on index cards can be provided by the teacher to the students. Everyone can then work together to put the information in correct categories on the chart.

Can be used as (1) the summarizing activity to a unit of study, (2) an ongoing activity, with a different group of students contributing

**Ancient Civilizations**

| Location: | Egypt | Greece | Rome | China | Mesopotamia |
|---|---|---|---|---|---|
| Map & Descr. | | | | | |
| Dates | | | | | |
| Major Cities | | | | | |
| Bordered by | | | | | |
| Rivers | | | | | |
| People | | | | | |
| Communication | | | | | |
| Customs | | | | | |
| Transportation | | | | | |

**Systems of Long-Distance Communication**

| Communication Type | Define | When | Where | How Long | Replaced By |
|---|---|---|---|---|---|
| Pony Express | | | | | Telegraph |
| Smoke Signals | | | | | Pony Express |
| Talking Drums | | | | | Smoke Signals |
| Telegraphs | | | | | Telephones |
| Telephones | | | | | Satellite Systems |

**Figure 8.2.**    *Sample information retrieval chart.*

information about one particular culture each week, or (3) an introduction or overview for a topic.

### Recommended Children's Books

Ganeri, A. (1997). *The Story of Communications.* Oxford University Press Incorporated.

Oliphant, M. (1993). *The Earliest Civilizations, Volume 1.* Facts on File Incorporated.

Schnidman, E. (2000). *Native American Answer Book.* Chelsea House Publishers.

Wood, A. (1992). *Errata: A Book of Historical Errors.* Stewart House.

### Technology Resources

www.500Nations.com/: Devoted to supplying information about indigenous Native American Populations.

www.smokesig.com/smk2sig.html#natamlks: A listing of many sites of interest for Native American culture and issues.

inventors.about.com/library/inventors/bl_history_of_communication.htm: A time line and description of the history of communication.

library.thinkquest.org/C004203/index2.htm: Time lines focusing on similarities and differences between today and the past in the areas of arts and culture, scientific discoveries, political organizations, social organizations, the world, economic organizations, economic organizations, and religions.

## EVERYTHING GOES DOWNSTREAM

Students will understand that actions taken by people aren't confined to their immediate area but affect people and locations "downstream" from where they live.

Duration: 1–3 class sessions
Group Size: small groups of 4 or 5
Disciplines: civics, ecology, geography, science, math
Skills: decision making, citizenship, responsible actions, inferring, values clarification
Key Vocabulary: wetlands, land use, pollution, environment, interdependence

Materials: 3 × 5 index cards, 8.5 × 11 paper, tape, glue sticks, scissors, crayons

## Procedure

1. Introduce the lesson by asking students what happens to the water when they wash their hands in the sink. Where does the water go? What happens to it? Where will it be used next? What is our source for fresh, clean water? What are the consequences of unwise use of water?

2. Group the students into teams of four students per team. Each team is to receive (a) a map of a relatively limited area (about 10 miles square) featuring a river that runs through the area, (b) 5 index cards, (c) scissors, and (d) tape or a glue stick. Directions for creating the map and features are located at the end of this activity.

3. Students arrange the created features (from the index cards) on their map in the manner each group decides is most appropriate to create a community. Roads and highways should be drawn in. Once arranged, the features will be taped or glued in place. Communities and pond should be given names.

4. Each group has a representative explain their map and why they arranged the items on the map in the manner they chose.

5. Maps are collected (as they are discussed) and taped to a wall in the classroom, with the river from one map connecting to the river of the next map until all maps form a long river.

6. Discussion that follows examines the consequences of what occurs both upstream and downstream and how the decisions from one community have an effect on all the other communities along the river.

## Extensions/Adaptations

- Students can role-play as members of special-interest groups, each of which has an agenda for a particular land use. Suggested groups follow: (1) land developers who wish to subdivide the land and sell the small parcels for home construction; (2) heavy industry that promises jobs for the people of the area in exchange for land on which their land-intensive (and dirty?) industry can locate; (3) farmers who want to have large areas available for grazing livestock and crop growth; (4) citizen groups who want areas for recreation including fishing, hiking, play areas, and sports; (5) governmental highway departments who want to develop major highways to allow increased access for the citizens of the area and for heavy trucks to travel through the area as well as for tourists who may wish to visit the area; (6) business interests who wish to develop shopping areas; (7) conservationists who want to preserve the natural areas for future generations and for present enjoyment.

- A suggested format is a mock town meeting where the relative merits of the projects from each special-interest group can be presented and debated by the class members.
- Illustrate the real-world significance of this activity using the Mississippi River as an example of a stream that must absorb and transport all sorts of materials from its headwaters and the population centers that lie along its shores as it flows southward into the Gulf of Mexico. How are the actions of people in Missouri of vital interest to the people along the banks of the Mississippi in Louisiana?

### Recommended Children's Books

Atwell, Debby. (1999). *River*. Houghton Mifflin.
Cainer, Margaret. (1992). *From the Mountains to the Sea: A Journey in Environmental Citizenship*. Environment Canada.
Cherry, Lynn. (1992). *A River Ran Wild*. Harcourt, Brace and Company.
Chester, M., & Micale, Al. (1969). *Let's Go to Stop Water Pollution*. Putnam.
Doiris, Arthur. (1991). *Follow the Water from Brook to Ocean*. Harper Collins.
Holling, Holling. (1980). *Paddle to the Sea*. Sandpiper Books.
Locker, Thomas. (1984). *Where the River Begins*. Penguin Books.

### Technology Resources

www.epa.gov/owow/nps/kids/: A U.S. Environmental Protection Service site for kids, concerning polluted runoff into streams and lakes.
www.kiddyhouse.com/Themes/Environ/Water.html: A listing of sites about water and pollution for kids and teachers.

www.oceansidecleanwaterprogram.org/kids.asp: How water becomes polluted and how individuals may help prevent this from happening.

## Creating the Map

On an 8.5 × 11-inch sheet of paper, draw a river (indicated by a wavy line) from the northeast quadrant of the page to the north/northeast quadrant. Adjacent to the river, place an irregular circle to indicate a pond. Insert several symbols at various locations to indicate trees. Duplicate this so that all students are presented with the same map on which to create their communities.

## Creating the Features

Have students cut five index cards into the sections and label each piece. They will then color and arrange the pieces on the map to complete each group's task. Index card #1 should be cut into halves, one half being a park and the other half being an airfield. Index card #2 should be cut into halves, with one half being a field in which a farmer would grow crops and the other half being a playground. Index card #3 should be cut into sixths. Each sixth is a house. Index card #4 should be cut into sixths. Each sixth is one of the following: gas station, grocery store, dry cleaner, pharmacy, post office, school. Index card #5 should be cut into halves, fourths, or sixths. Students identify other features that will be in their created communities.

# CHAPTER 9

# Global Connections

This sure doesn't look like Kansas anymore . . .

—Dorothy from *The Wizard of Oz*

Understanding global connections is a concept related to all other social studies standards. Today, virtually everything we do has global connections: the foods we eat, the clothes we wear, the cars we drive, our furniture, medicines, electronics are all obtained from various countries around the world. There are few facets of normal existence that remain in complete isolation within today's global community. To understand the complex interrelationships among various components of contemporary life, one needs to appreciate the presence of the many worldwide connections found in the local community. Often related to the concept of current events in school settings, global-connection activities and strategies provide students with opportunities to examine and analyze relationships among and between countries, people, cultures, natural resources, climates, and topographies of world areas. Students must gather and analyze information from various media sources about current news and issues related to entities within the global community, including historical perspectives. As with most things, students need to have knowledge about the world farther afield than their immediate community, town, state, or nation if they are to be informed global citizens. All disciplines can provide experiences through which students can learn about global events and the way these events affect their lives and those of others.

## THE TRIP

In groups, students will serve as travel agents and plan a trip to a foreign country for the month of December.

Duration: approximately 1 week

Group Size: 4 groups of appropriate size, or more groups if group tasks are redistributed.

Skills: organization, classification, inference, prediction

Disciplines: geography, economics, language arts, mathematics

Key Vocabulary: itinerary, foreign exchange rate, words identified by various groups

Materials: Australian map, world map, pencils, paper, resource materials

### Procedure

1. Divide students into four groups, as defined in the next section, to plan a trip to Sydney, Australia.
2. Groups share information with other groups. Selections are made by each group and consolidated into booklet form. Each group shares end results with the class.
3. Focus on the aspect of a summer holiday season (Christmas, Chanukah) in the southern hemisphere, commercial aspects of the holiday, and/or the length of the celebration. Each group plots on maps the routes to be taken and sites to be visited.

### Groups 1–4

1. This group will plan the flight itinerary for the trip. They will work with Internet sites or online travel agencies to obtain information about flights to Sydney, the time and the day they would leave their city, the airports where they would land, where they (might) change planes, how many hours the flight would take, and the time and day on which they would arrive in Sydney. They should determine how long the flight takes and why the day

changes when they fly from their city to Sydney. This group will also do the same for the trip from Sydney to their home city. Any plane changes in either direction should be identified. Baggage restrictions should be included, necessary passport information identified, and means of transportation arranged for when they arrive in Sydney. The group should provide three or four different possible itineraries so that individuals in the class will be able to decide among them.

2. Information about vacationing in Australia should be obtained by this group from the Internet, library, and/or writing to the Australian Consulate-General (1 Bush Street, San Francisco, CA 94104-4413). All information should be obtained in hard copy so others in the class may examine it carefully. This group should also collect information about seasonal vacation pursuits that differ between the two countries at this time of year.

3. Group three will determine the rate of exchange between Australian dollars and local currency and identify where and how money can be converted to Australian dollars. They should also find out the cost of hotels and other goods and services in Sydney. Comparisons between Australian and U.S. dollars should be made.

4. This group should locate information on how Christmas, Chanukah, and the like are celebrated in Sydney, as well as how these celebrations in Sydney differ from those in their home city. Information can be obtained through the Internet, magazines, books, and travel guides.

**Extensions/Adaptations**

- Select any country in the world to visit.
- Address language differences: mate (friend), brumby (horse), billabong (watering hole), and so on.
- Have different groups of students work on different countries. Once all of the presentations have been made, allow the class to vote on where they would most like to visit.
- Have students plan their trips based on the assumption that the group is traveling from a location other than the home location to a foreign location (e.g., Innsbruck, Austria, to Moscow, Russia).

- Exchange some U.S. money for foreign currency at a bank for use as a visual during this activity. It can sometimes take several days, so the request should be made in advance.
- Obtain posters and pamphlets from a local travel agency to supplement the information obtained by the students and to provide student motivation and interest.
- Extend the activity through examination of day trips into other areas of Australia.

## Recommended Children's Books

Ajmera, Maya K. (1997). *Children from Australia to Zimbabwe*. Charlesbridge Publishing Inc.

DK Travel Writers. (2000). *Eyewitness Travel Guide: Sydney*. Dorling Kindersley Limited.

Edward, George. (2004). *Code Word Kangaroo*. Random House.

Heinrichs, Ann. (1998). *Australia*. Children's Press.

Petersen, D. (1998 & 1999). *Continents True Books Series*. Children's Press.

## Technology Resources

www.lonelyplanet.com/destinations/australasia/australia/: A description of Australia, basic statistics, and links to a variety of relevant information.

www.about-australia.com/about.htm: Facts and links about the various territories of Australia.

onlineedition.culturerams.com: The daily life and cultures, including history, customs, and lifestyles, of the world's people.

www.pacificislandtravel.com/australia/about_destin/people.esp: Information and pictures about many facets of Australian life.

## NEWS FROM AROUND THE WORLD

While collecting newspaper articles, students will make connections on a world map among locations affected by the news item.

Duration: approximately one week

Group Size: varies

Skills: organization, classification, inference, prediction,

Disciplines: language arts, mathematics, all social studies areas
Key Vocabulary: varies according to news items
Materials: world map, newspaper articles, yarn in two or more colors, pushpins or stapler, newspapers

**Procedure**

1. Divide into three or four groups. Each group will be assigned a newspaper section or topic (local news, sports, weather, historical item, etc.) to locate within the newspaper.
2. Each person in each group locates an article and shares it with others in the group. Each group then selects one article from those located to share with the class. Before sharing, each group finds news locations on a map.
3. Each group presents to the rest of the class the content of the article and identifies from where the news item originated. Each article is attached to bulletin board (offset map). Yarn is used to link the article to the primary article location on the map. (The same color should always be used to link articles with primary location).
4. Lead a class discussion on the impact of the news item on other parts of the world. Link news item with these locations by using another color of yarn between the article and these other locations.
5. Repeat for all articles. Continue for several days, leaving all items on the bulletin board until space is too limited. Before removing all items and beginning the procedure again, discuss the links that have been made around the world.

**Extensions/Adaptations**

- Headlines of newspaper articles, rather than the entire article, can be used on the bulletin board to save space.
- Newspaper articles can be brought from home by a specified number of students each day, and connections can be made together by the class during the morning routine.
- A daily article can be identified by the teacher and brought in to be discussed. Daily articles can address a different topic (sports, weather, headlines, etc.) each day.

## Recommended Children's Books

Brown, Don. (2004). *Kid Blink Beats the World*. Roaring Brook Press.

Christensen, Bonnie. (2003). *The Daring Nellie Blye*. Alfred A. Knopf.

Englart, Mindi Rose. (2001). *Newspapers from Start to Finish*. Gale Group.

George, Lindsay Barrett. (1999). *Around the World: Who's Been There*. Greenwillow Press.

Hamilton, John. (2004). *Newspapers*. ABDO Publishers.

National Geographic Society. (2003). *National Geographic Atlas for Young Explorers*. National Geographic Society.

## Technology Resources

www.worldnews.com/: A comprehensive global news network.

www.csun.edu/~hcedu013/cevents.html: Teaching current events via newspapers, magazines, and television.

www.kidscoop.com: A newspaper activity page with activities and information for students, teachers, and parents.

## KAMISHIBAI STORY CARDS

Students will demonstrate comprehension, practice oral and written communication skills, and develop visual and spatial knowledge through the construction of a Japanese storytelling tool.

Duration: 1–3 days

Group Size: groups of 5–6

Skills: organization, classification, inference, prediction,

Disciplines: geography, history, language arts, mathematics

Key Vocabulary: Kamishibai, Japan, tradition

Materials: one 12 × 18-inch tag board rectangle per student, crayons, markers, paint

### Procedure

1. Share the history of Kamishibai (kah-mee-shee-bye), located in the section at the end of this activity. Locate Japan on a world map. Share and model a Kamishibai story. Discuss the story and

have students identify the primary story components (title, character, setting, problem, problem resolution, theme).

2. Show how the text and illustrations of Kamishibai are arranged.
3. Read a fiction or nonfiction story related to the social studies topic being studied. Identify the most important parts of the story.
4. Divide the class into groups and assign each student in the group one part of the story to illustrate on a piece of tag board.
5. Have each group of students practice retelling the story in sequence, using dialogue as well as narration. Each student tells his or her part of the story and displays the story card.
6. Have each student write his or her part of the story on a sheet of paper. Arrange the students sequentially within groups and have each transfer his or her part of the story onto the back of the appropriate card, numbering the cards as they complete the transference. The text for the first illustrated story card is on the back of the last card; the text for the second illustrated story card is on the back of the first story card; the text for the third illustrated story card is on the back of the second story card, and so on.
7. Encourage one student per group to share the entire set of cards with the rest of the class, reading and displaying the appropriate cards.
8. Place all cards from each group in individually labeled envelopes. Place these envelopes in the reading area of the classroom.

### Extension/Adaptations

- Have individuals create an entire set of cards—either an original story, a researched topic, or a summary of a book they have just completed reading.
- Discuss how this form of reader's theater can be implemented with stories found in books. Model an example and have students create one of their own.

### Recommended Children's Books

Amos, Berthe. (1994). *The Cajun Gingerbread Boy*. Hyperion Books for Children. (South Louisiana version of "The Gingerbread Boy")
Friedman, Ira R. (1987). *How My Parents Learned to Eat*. Houghton Mifflin.
Khanduri, Kamini. (2003). *Japanese Art and Culture*. Raintree Press.

Laird, D. M. (1985). *'Ula Li'i and the Magic Shark*. Barnaby Books. (Hawaiian version of "Little Red Riding Hood")

Laird, Donivee Martin. (1982). *Keaka and the Lilikoi Vine*. Barnaby Books. (Hawaiian version of "Jack and the Beanstalk").

Littlefield, Holly. (2003). *The Color of Japan*. Bt. Bound Publishers.

Lowell, Susan. (1992). *The Three Little Javelinas*. Northland Publishing. (Southwestern version of "The Three Little Pigs")

Reynolds, Jeff. (2004). *Japan (A to Z)*. Children's Press.

Say, Allen. (1993). *Grandfather's Journey*. Houghton Mifflin.

Say, Allen. (1999). *Tea with Milk*. Houghton Mifflin.

Turner, Pamela S. (2004). *Hachiko: The True Story of a Loyal Dog*. Houghton Mifflin.

### Technology Resources

www.kamishibai.com: Kamishibai for children.

www.indiana.edu/~japan/kamishibai: A Kamishibai play for students with links to other Kamishibai sites.

www.princeton.edu/~cotsen/outreach/resources/act_kamishibai.html: The history of Kamishibai and recommendations for uses.

### The History of Kamishibai (kah-mee-shee-bye)

Prior to 1953 (when television arrived in Japan), itinerant storytellers would ride into towns on a bicycle. Once the storyteller arrived in the center of the village, the people of the area would hear the sound of two wooden blocks being struck together announcing his arrival. First, he would sell candy, and those who bought candy from the Kamishibai got to sit in the front row for storytelling. Using hand-illustrated story cards, the Kamishibai would entertain those present with stories, often stopping right at a pivotal point in the story and leaving for another village, promising to return in a few days to complete the story and begin a new one.

## CULTURAL ENCOUNTER

Through a simulation, students will experience entering a foreign culture where they are unable to communicate in English with the local population.

Duration: 1–2 days
Group Size: 2 groups—size varies
Skills: organization, classification, inference, prediction
Disciplines: sociology, anthropology, language arts
Key Vocabulary: tone sticks, foreign, belief systems, culture
Materials: one set of pick-up sticks, cultural encounter discussion
   sheet

## Procedure

1. Divide the class into two teams. Move the two groups to separate spaces and prepare—one leader working with the "Teh-myongs" to learn their culture and the other leader working with the "students" to devise strategies for getting to know this foreign population. Divide the pick-up sticks among the two groups with the "Teh-myongs" getting most of the sticks, including the black one and at least two red ones.

2. Direct the leader of the "Teh-myongs" to teach the population their habits (see "Teh-myong Information" later in this section) and to monitor during engagement between the two groups.

3. Direct the "student" leader to say, "All I can tell you for sure is that you will be the first foreigners to meet these people. I do not know anything about them except that they like pick-up sticks. Here are a few you can use as you think best." This group should consider the following:
   • They do not speak Teh-myong.
   • What will be their primary purpose as they first enter the culture?
   • What are some guidelines they will follow when meeting and greeting this unknown group?
   • What will they do with the pick-up sticks?

4. Allow for the following:
   a. Ten minutes for the training phase.
   b. Five to ten minutes for the first engagement between the groups.
   c. Five minutes following disengagement to allow for discussion.
   d. Five to ten minutes for the second engagement.

e. The remainder of the time will be used for whole-group de-
briefing using the information provided under "Cultural
Encounter Discussion," near the end of this section: Give im-
pressions of the other culture; state the perceived belief system
of the other culture; discuss events, actions, and feelings generated by the encounter; and make links between this experience and traveling to a foreign land.

## Extensions/Adaptations

* To change the activity, redistribute the sticks for various engage-
ments. (For example, decrease the number of sticks to fewer sticks
than people, students have all the sticks, "Teh-myongs" have all
the sticks, "Choo-ja" [see "Teh-myong Information"] starts with
all the sticks, etc.).
* The information for the "Teh-myongs" can be used in its entirety
or can be severely limited, based on the abilities of the students.

## Recommended Children's Books

Ajmera, Maya. (2001). *Children from Australia to Zimbabwe*. Charlesbridge
Publications Incorporated.

Fox, Mem. (2001). *Whoever You Are*. Harcourt Brace and Company.

Haven, Kendall. (1999). *New Year's to Kwanza: Original Stories of Celebration*. Fulcrum Publishers.

Menzel, Peter. (1995). *Material World: A Global Family Portrait*. Sierra Club
Books.

Smith, David J. (2002). *If the World Were a Village: A Book about the World's
People*. Kids Can Press.

Spier, Peter. (1988). *People*. Doubleday Books for Young Readers.

## Technology Resources

www.princeton.edu/~cotsen/outreach/resources/act_kamishibai.html: Resources for indigenous cultures around the world.

www.school-library.org/pathfinders/Davis_CulturesAroundtheWorld.pdf:
Pathfinder to use for a research tool when learning about various cultures.

www.culturegrams.com: Daily life and culture, including history, customs, and
lifestyles, of people of the world, with links to teacher's and children's sites.

**Teh-myong Information**

The Teh-myongs spend their lives collecting and giving away their tone sticks. These sticks are like social currency and may be traded for favors or held to bring honor to the holder. The darker the stick, the higher the value.

For example, a handshake could be considered as a trading gesture: "Who needs a tone stick?" "Hi" means I would like one. "No" means I do not wish to take one from you, or you may not take one from me. "Low" means to please take the lowest value of stick I have.

If you shake hands with someone and say "Hi," you may take one of their sticks if they do not say "No." If you both say "Hi," you exchange sticks.

- The Teh-myongs greet each other with a bow. If someone fails to bow to one having sticks, it is considered rude, and usually the stick holder wags an index finger at the offender saying "Ahn-dway" (meaning shameful) and walks away.
- The more sticks one has, the greater the respect and the deeper the bow one receives.
- If someone holds three sticks, they are "Teh-jong" and must be honored with a bow and the greeting "Teh-jong" when met. The Teh-jong walks away from those who fail to do this.
- A person holding a black stick is considered the "Choo-ja," or leader, and when this person says "Choo-ja'sah," others within hearing distance give him or her one stick and place their right hands in front of their lips and bow. Anyone holding a red stick is responsible for taking anyone not showing respect to the Choo-ja to the farthest edge of the assembly, wagging an index finger at the offender, and walking away.
- The Choo-ja usually gives a stick to everyone he or she meets if any are available. If only the black stick remains, the Choo-ja usually looks for someone with many sticks and gives them the black one in exchange for one of any other color, thus establishing a new Choo-ja. A Choo-ja may, but does not have to, follow any established customs.
- Persons can do as they wish with their sticks: hide them, give them away to friends, or leave them on the ground.

- The Teh-myong do not understand English. They respond to strangers with friendly enthusiasm and are generally very good-natured. They can only speak to strangers through sign and stick-trading language. They tend to shun people who demonstrate an inability to share tone sticks. They may speak to one another when strangers are not around, but become silent when one approaches.

The following are parts of the Teh-Myong vocabulary:

Teh-jong = rich one.
Choo-ja'sah = leader offering.
Hi = May I have one?
No = no.
Ahn-dway = shameful.
Hi-keen-no = Take a low one.
Low = Take stick with lowest value.

**Cultural Encounter Discussion**
*Copyright 2002, Dara Wakefield, Rome, GA*

1. Did you feel accepted or unaccepted (as either an insider or an outsider) during the activity?
2. List three feelings you had.
3. What happened to make you feel this way?
4. List three feelings you think "they" had.
5. What did you first do when entering the new culture?
6. What would you do differently next time?
7. If you were visiting another country where the people did not speak your language, what could you do to become accepted? Would you ever become an "insider" in that culture? Why or why not?

## CONNECTING THROUGH GAMES

By playing games that originated in various locations around the world, students will become more aware of similarities and differences between their homes and distant locations.

Duration: several days
Group Size: varies
Skills: organization, classification, inference, prediction
Disciplines: sociology, mathematics, anthropology, physical education
Key Vocabulary: varies dependent upon game
Materials: varies dependent upon game

## Procedure

1. Choose one or more of the books listed. Share the book aloud with the class. Discuss with students similarities and differences of the cultural aspects or people depicted in the books. Have students provide examples of similarities and differences among the various books and between the books' contents and themselves. Examine the illustrations and discuss similarities and differences.
2. Using the list of books that focus on games around the world, have students participate in playing several games. Compare and contrast each of the games with similar games in the United States (e.g., Jan Ken Pon in Japan is similar to rock-paper-scissors in the United States).

## Extension/Adaptation

Engage students in cooking foods from around the world. Compare and contrast the foods with local foods. Extend to various ethnic and regional foods within the one particular country (e.g., Louisiana's Cajun cooking, Louisiana's Creole cooking, Texas's Tex-Mex cooking, etc.)

## Recommended Children's Books

Braman, Arlette N. (2002). *Kids around the World Play*. Wiley Publishers.
DK Publishing. *A Life Like Mine*. (2002). Dorling Kindersley Publishing.
Dunn, Opel. (2000). *Acha Bacha Boo!: Playground Games from around the World*. Henry Holt and Company.
Flanagan, Alice. (2003). *Chinese New Year*. Compass Point Books.
Flanagan, Alice. (2003). *Carnival*. Compass Point Books.

Flanagan, Alice. (2003). *Cinco de Mayo*. Compass Point Books.

Hall, Godfrey. (1995). *Games (Traditions around the World)*. Steck Vaughn.

Haskins, Jim. (1992). *Count Your Way through Africa*. Carolrhoda Books.

Johnson, Anne Akers. (1996). *String Games from around the World*. Klutz Press.

Kindersley, Barbara. (1997). *Celebrations*. DK Publishing.

Kindersley, Barbara. (1995). *Children Just Like Me*. DK Publishing.

Lankford, Mary. (2000). *Birthdays around the World*. William Morrow and Company.

Lankford, Mary. (1992). *Hopscotch around the World*. New York: Morrow Junior Books.

Milord, Susan. (1999). *Hands around the World*. Gareth Stevens Audio.

Montana, Donata. (2001). *Children around the World*. Kids Can Press, Ltd.

Zaslavsky, Claudia. (1998). *Math Games and Activities from around the World*. Chicago Review Press.

Zaslavsky, Claudia. (2003). *More Math Games and Activities from around the World*. Chicago Review Press.

## Technology Resources

www.topics-mag.com/edition11/games-section.htm: Photos of and directions for games children play around the world.

ky.essortment.com/gameforchild_rwnd.htm: Directions for children's games from around the globe, focusing on African, Cuban, French, and Zuni games.

www.communityschool.net/childeren's_games.htm: Links to directions for board games of the ancient world, games and sports played around the world, and international games.

# CHAPTER 10

# Civic Ideals and Practices

You have brains in your head. You have feet in your shoes. You can steer yourself. Any direction you choose.

—Dr. Seuss

Civic ideals are beliefs held by individuals, such as belief in the rights and responsibilities of people in society or in the promotion of the ideals of a country's government. Civic ideals and practices knowledge can focus on participation in civic affairs, such as elections or community service, and emphasize the ideas of personal, political, and economic responsibilities.

Students should be able to demonstrate how citizens use societal knowledge when responding to daily life in a democracy, working with others, expressing ideas, and managing conflict. Demonstration of civic knowledge generally occurs in seven basic areas: civic life; politics; government; foundations of the political system; how the government represents the purposes, values, and principles of American democracy (as established in the Constitution); the relationship of the United States to other countries and their governments; and the roles of citizens in American democracy. Through identification, description, explanation, and analysis of information, students can evaluate specific events in society that impact everyday life and can make global connections for the effects of these events. Best addressed through the disciplines of history, political science, sociology, and psychology, civic ideals and practices are considered a central purpose of all social studies areas and should emphasize the individual's role in society as well as that of groups and institutions.

## PRIORITIZING RESPONSIBILITY

Each student within groups is provided with a set of civic responsibility cards that are prioritized by individuals and then discussed as groups attempt to arrive at consensus regarding what makes a good citizen.

Duration: one class period
Group Size: individual and small groups
Disciplines: philosophy, political science, sociology, language arts, civics
Skills: describing, generalizing, classifying, evaluating, analyzing
Key Vocabulary: citizenship, responsibility
Materials: one set of civic responsibility cards per student (items should be written on index cards using the same set of items for each group)

## Procedure

*Part 1*

1. Discuss citizenship and develop a web on the board, chart paper, or overhead on which students' examples of citizenship are classified. Discuss: Why do we all have different ideas about what is involved in being a good citizen? Who is right? Why?
2. Distribute two sets of responsibility cards to a small group of students. The exact card set used depends on students' prior knowledge and student age and grade level. Place the cards face down on a table. When all cards are placed face down, students take turns trying to turn over "matches."

*Part 2*

1. Provide individuals with one set of cards. Have students arrange the cards into a row or column. The cards should be arranged from what they consider most important (top or left) to least important (bottom or right).

2. As a class, discuss placement of the various cards on individual lists: Why do we all have different ideas about what is involved in being a good citizen? Who is right? Why? Have students determine in their groups if there is a responsibility that is not included in the cards that should be included. Have groups discuss their reasons for the importance of various items.

**Extensions/Adaptations**

- Make duplicate sets of cards and develop them into a card game for use with three to four children. Children will make sets of matching cards.
- When students have completed the part 2 task, divide the class into groups of about three or four. Have students discuss the order in which they each placed their cards, starting with the first card on the stack. Each student should provide a reason for placing the card at the specific spot. All reasons for placing cards at a particular place in the card stack should be accepted. Once all of the cards have been discussed in the group, the group should attempt to come to a consensus about the two most important components of civic responsibility. Groups share the top two components with the rest of the class, then the bottom two components. Discuss what happens to the organization of the cards if the new items are included.
- Enlarge one set of cards and place them on the board (attach with tape). Have students discuss each card and attempt to organize them in order of importance. This should be difficult to do, which will allow for discussion about how the relative importance of each item is a personal decision.

**Recommended Children's Books**

Berenstain, Jan, & Berenstain, Stan. (1997). *The Berenstain Bears and the Blame Game*. Random House.

Berenstain, Jan, & Berenstain, Stan. (1988). *The Berenstain Bears and the Truth*. Random House.

Berenstain, Jan, & Berenstain, Stan. (1999). *The Berenstain Bears Think about Those in Need*. Random House.

Brown, Marc. (1999). *Arthur's Computer Disaster*. Little, Brown and Company.

Garay, Luis. (1997). *Pedrito's Day*. Orchard Books.

Napoli, Donna Jo. (2000). *Running Away*. Aladdin Paperbacks.

Sachar, Louis. (1994). *Alone in His Teacher's House*. Random Library.

**Technology Resources**

www.pbs.org/wnet/newyork/laic/: "Learning Adventures in Citizenship" for young students.

www.cewc-cymru.org.uk/: The council for education in world citizenship works with young people to promote active global citizenship.

www.usoe.k12.ut.us/curr/lifeskills/resp.html: Lists attributes of a responsible citizen.

**Civic Responsibility Cards: Set 1**

| | |
|---|---|
| Following Rules | Honesty |
| Cleanliness | Trustworthiness |
| Kindness | Fairness |
| Caring | Friendship |
| Responsibility | Respect |

**Civic Responsibility Cards: Set 2**

| | |
|---|---|
| Cleaning your room | Washing or drying dishes |
| Making your bed | Sweeping/vacuuming the floor |
| Brushing your teeth | Feeding or walking the pet |
| Taking out the trash | Getting up on time |
| Setting the table | Helping take care of your brother or sister |

**Civic Responsibility Cards: Set 3**

| | |
|---|---|
| Voting for public officials | Helping people who are in need |
| Working to eliminate violence | Helping keep the environment clean |
| Being aware of world events | Having and keeping a job |
| Having an active social life | Helping unwanted pets find a home |

## GROUP PROBLEM SOLVING

Given situation cards that describe situations relevant to students today, groups of students discuss possible solutions and consequences as well as the idea that there may sometimes be more than one correct answer.

Duration: 1 class period
Group Size: small groups of 5
Disciplines: sociology, psychology, political science, philosophy
Skills: evaluating, interpreting, analyzing, deducing, hypothesizing, inferring
Key Vocabulary: roles, responsibility, participation, characteristics, honesty, respect, fairness, concern, choices, consequences, compromise
Materials: scenario cards—one set per group

**Procedure**

Prior to activity: Duplicate the scenario-card information and glue each to an index card so each group will have one set of cards.

*Part 1*

1. Discuss the following terms: honesty, respect, responsibility, fairness, and concern. Have students provide examples and nonexamples for each term. Discuss the concept "All choices are personal decisions." One must realize that for every choice, there is a consequence. Consequences can be positive or negative. Discuss the phrase "Agree to disagree."

2. Place a transparency of the problem-solving discussion format on the overhead projector and discuss the various components: identifying the problem, thinking of possible solutions, taking different points of view, possible compromises, selecting an option.

3. Divide the class into groups and provide each group with one set of scenario cards and a copy of the problem-solving discussion format. Assign responsibilities for each person in the group:

    a. Problem reader—Reads the problem aloud to the group.

    b. Problem identifier—Relates the problem in his or her own words to the group.

    c. Alternate viewpoint provider—Presents the problem from the point of view of someone other than the main character in the problem.

    d. Solution indicator—Identifies solutions in addition to those listed on the card.

    e. Compromiser—Provides a compromise solution.

4. Provide a copy of the directions to each group or place it on the overhead for reference.

## Directions for Scenario Cards

1. Shuffle the cards and place them in the center of the group.
2. The problem reader selects one card and reads it to him- or herself and then reads it aloud to the group.
3. Allow about two minutes for everyone to think about the possible responses.
4. Each person responds according to his or her identified responsibility.
5. Each person should then select an option and identify why he or she made that particular choice. All choices are valid as long as a logical rationale for the choice is provided.
6. After completing the first card, responsibilities should shift clockwise so that each person has a different role for the new card.
7. Monitor groups closely to ensure that all choices are provided proper respect by others in the group, especially when there is disagreement among group members.

## Extensions/Adaptations

- Rather than many small groups, assign a specific card to each group and then have each group share their experiences and opinions with the class OR allow each group to randomly select a card to discuss and share with the class OR work on each card as an entire class and provide opportunities for everyone to express opinions and rationale.

- Develop cards with simpler problems for use with younger children: sharing candy or toys with others, using someone's things without first asking, helping others with a problem, and so on.
- Construct a problem-solving flow chart for the students to use as a reference as they work through problems.
- Have students identify character traits associated with each problem-solving card: trustworthiness, fairness, and so on.
- Have students develop new and additional cards based on situations of which they are aware in their communities or at school.

### Recommended Children's Books

Coleman, Penny. (1991). *Dark Closets and Noises in the Night*. Paulist Press.
Conner, Catherine. (1996). *Alison Saves the Wedding*. Magic Attic Press.
Dilaura, Cynthia. (1993). *The Wind before It Blows*. Abdo and Daughters Press.
Garvey, Linda K. (1999). *Doug Cheats*. Disney Press.
Javernick, Ellen. (1995). *Ms. Pollywog's Problem-Solving Service*. Augsburg Fortress Publishers.
Krulik, Nancy. (1999). *Doug Rules*. Disney Press.
Williams, L. E. (1999). *Island Rose*. Magic Attic Press.

### Technology Resources

www.playkidsgames.com/problem_solveGames.htm: A series of problem-solving games.
www.bnet.org/hvsd/design.briefs/problem.htm: A series of problems for students to solve using common household items.
www.glencoe.com/sec/busadmin/entire/teacher/creative: A series of links and examples in problems solving.

### Problem-Solving Discussion Format

*Identify the Problem*

1. In your own words, state the problem.
2. Who does the problem affect?
3. What are any other problems involved?
4. Who are any other people involved in the problem?

*Possible Solutions*

1. What are three or four different ways the problem could be resolved?
2. What are the advantages to each of these ways?
3. What are the disadvantages to each of these ways?
4. Will any of these solutions cause new or additional problems? If so, what are those problems?
5. Do the solutions really solve the problem, or do they just help someone avoid the problem or postpone having to deal with the problem for a while?
6. Are there any people who could provide help in solving the problem?

*Alternate Viewpoints*

1. How will each person involved with the problem be affected by the solutions?
2. How will anyone else be affected by the solutions to the problem?
3. How would you feel if you were the person involved in the problem and this solution were implemented?
4. If you were the person involved in the problem, what would you do?
5. If your best friend were the person involved in the problem, how would you want the issue to be resolved?

*Compromise*

1. Are there any ways your solutions can be combined so that a compromise situation can occur?
2. If so, what solutions will work best together?
3. If not, why will none of the solutions work together?
4. Does the compromise situation really take care of the problem, or does it just postpone having to take action?
5. Does a compromise enable all people involved in the problem to be positively affected?

*Selecting an Option*

1. Of all the solutions suggested and possible compromises, in your opinion which do you think is best?
2. What is your rationale for selecting that option?
3. Provide an oral (or written) summary of your option and reason and what you believe will happen as a result of this decision.

*Scenario-Card Information*

Carlos has been tutoring some third graders in reading after school. He doesn't want to do it anymore because none of his friends tutor. Should he:

- just not show up anymore?
- tell his parents that he isn't needed to tutor anymore?
- tell his teacher that his parents say he can't stay after school to tutor any longer?
- other?

Angelina has started going to a new school after moving to a new city. The group of girls she has started hanging out with want her to join their gang. Should she:

- join the gang so she can make new friends?
- tell them she is already a member of a gang in the city from which she moved?
- hang out with the gang at school only but not after school?
- other?

Tom needs to make at least a C on his American history test or he'll be dropped from the football team. He didn't study as much as he should have, and so he asked his best friend Jack to help him with some of the answers during the test. Should Jack:

- give Tom all of the answers?
- give Tom some of the answers?
- convince Tom to talk to the teacher about the importance of him staying on the football team?

- tell Tom that if he didn't study he doesn't belong on the football team?
- other

Kalandra's grandmother has come to live with her family. Her grandmother likes to tell stories about the times when she was a girl every time Kalandra's friends come by to visit. Kalandra's friends think the grandmother is a crazy lady and make fun of her when she's not looking. Should Kalandra:

- get new friends?
- tell her friends they are being mean?
- agree with her friends when she's not at home with her grandmother?
- other?

Justine has always been interested in computers and has never worried about popularity like many of her friends. One day she comes to school to find the word "geek" written in large red letters across her locker. Now she doesn't want to attend this school anymore because of what the other students must think of her. Should she:

- not worry about it and go to school anyway?
- convince her parents to let her transfer to another school?
- get more involved in other types of activities instead of computers?
- other?

Maria's parents are upset about the graffiti that has been painted on the outside of an apartment building in their neighborhood. They ask Maria if she knows who did it, and she tells them "no." Even though she watched the graffiti being painted, she didn't do any of the painting herself, and she thinks it looks great. Should Maria:

- tell her parents who did it?
- call the police about the graffiti painters?
- try to convince the graffiti painters not to paint any more?
- other?

Antonio's neighbor, Mr. Griggs, seems lonely. His wife died last year, and he doesn't have any children or grandchildren. Anytime Anthony tries to talk to Mr. Griggs, Mr. Griggs always seems grumpy. Should Anthony:

- not try to engage Mr. Griggs in conversation anymore since it hasn't done any good so far?
- keep trying and smiling?
- do something nice for Mr. Griggs without him knowing about it?
- other

Danielle has been taking care of her neighbors' fish while the neighbors are out of town. She came down with a stomach "bug" for a couple of days and forgot about them. When she remembered and went to feed them, one of the fish had died. Should she:

- call the neighbors and tell them that one of the fish got sick and died?
- hope the neighbors don't notice they no longer have one of the fish?
- wait until the neighbors get home before telling them that one of the fish got sick and died?
- other?

## YOU AND THE CONSTITUTION

Students will understand how rules are developed and why people who work and play together should follow rules.

Duration: 1 class period
Group Size: small groups of 5
Disciplines: sociology, psychology, political science, history
Skills: evaluating, interpreting, analyzing, deducing, inferring
Key Vocabulary: rules, laws, constitution, welfare, rights
Materials: copy of the U.S. Constitution, camera (Polaroid w/film or digital), colored construction paper, colored chart paper

**Procedure**

1. Introduce the topic by asking the following questions: What do you celebrate on your birthday? (the anniversary of your birth); What other kinds of anniversaries call for celebrations? (weddings, special occasions); What does our country celebrate on the Fourth of July? (its birthday—the anniversary of the founding of the United States of America). Discuss that the United States is over 200 years old and that once it became a country, it needed rules to follow. Show a copy of the U.S. Constitution. Explain that this document contains the laws of the United States and lists our country's rules and the rights of its citizens.

2. Have students give opinions about how people who lived in the United States 200 years ago might have dressed, the kinds of homes in which they lived, and the kinds of schools students might have attended. Take full-length photographs of each other. Discuss: How do the people in these photos (you) differ from people who lived in 1787? How do they look similar? Look at things around the classroom or school and identify the TV, telephone, automobile, computer, book, and so on and discuss which objects would be familiar to people who lived 200 years ago. Which would be unfamiliar? Why? Do you think anyone took photographs of the men who wrote the Constitution? Why not? If photographs had been taken, what do you think they would have shown? If people met today to make changes in the Constitution, could there be photos of the meetings? What might be in the photos to let you know they were taken in the 2000s and not in the 1700s? Ask students to read the first three words ("We the people . . .") of the Constitution. What do the words mean to you? If you could take one photograph to show the meaning of the words, what would be in the photograph? Discuss various ideas and have students design ways to take photographs of themselves illustrating these items.

3. Take a walking tour of the school in action (classroom, hallways, lunchroom, playground, etc.) Discuss what students observe. What are the rules for the various spaces within the school? How did they come about? Are they good or bad rules? Who decides if

they are good or bad? What or whom do they protect? Why do
you think we have rules? If you play a game for the first time,
how do you know how the game should be played? (Learn the
rules.) Why is it wrong to run in the school hallways? (It is
against school rules.) Through discussion, help students understand that rules give order, ensure fair play, and protect people's
rights and welfare.

**Extensions/Adaptations**

- Help students make a bulletin board of specific classroom procedures entitled "Do the Right Thing." If needed, subheadings can
  read as follows: "Working Quietly," "Cleaning Up," "Waiting to
  Speak," "Playing Fairly," "Asking Permission," "Raising Your
  Hand," "Sharing," "Using Equipment," and "Taking Turns." Have
  students draw pictures to illustrate each of the subheads. Display
  the drawings on the bulletin board to create a visual reference.
- Read *We The Kids*. Write a "Classroom Constitution" or "Kids
  Preamble" by having students suggest rules that will help make
  things run smoothly in the classroom. As each rule is proposed,
  have the class vote on whether or not it should be included in the
  document. If two-thirds or more votes yes, the rule becomes a part
  of the constitution. If not, the rule cannot be passed. Focus on
  things to be done in the classroom (raise your hand) rather than on
  what isn't desirable (don't yell out answers).
- Discussion topics: (1) Should students be allowed to bring any
  kind of toy to use at recess? What kinds should be allowed? What
  kinds should not be allowed? (2) Should there be a "court system"
  to judge students who break rules? How many judges should there
  be? Should all class members take turns being judges? What
  would be a reasonable punishment for breaking rules?
- Have students observe various sports or other activities where
  safety devices are evident. Discuss the special equipment needed as
  protection while playing certain sports (basketball, football, soccer,
  etc.). Ask: What do you use to protect yourself when it is very cold
  outside? Who are the people who protect you from harm? (parents,
  firefighters, police officers, government officials, and so on).

- Draw an analogy for students: the Constitution protects their rights just as an umbrella protects them from rain. Discuss symbols: a symbol is a picture, sign, sound, or object that stands for something else. Discuss U.S. symbols. Why might an umbrella be a good symbol for the Constitution? Discuss other symbols that could be used in place of an umbrella.

## Recommended Children's Books

Barnes, Peter, & Barnes, Cheryl. (1996). *House Mouse, Senate Mouse*. Rosebud Books.
Catrow, David. (2002). *We the Kids*. Dial Books.
Jordan, Terry. (1999). *The U.S. Constitution: And Fascinating Facts About It*. Oak Hall Publishing Company.
Krull, Kathleen. (1999). *A Kid's Guide to America's Bill of Rights*. Harper Collins.
Sobel, Syl, & Gilgannon, Denise. (2001). *The U.S. Constitution and You*. Barron's Educational Series.
Spier, Peter. (1987). *We the People*. Doubleday Books for Young Readers.

## Technology Resources

www.usconstitution.net/constkids.html: The constitution explained for kids K–3.
www.constitutioncenter.org/explore/ForKids/index.shtml: Facts and activities for children concerning the U.S. Constitution.
www.house.gov/pombo/kids/trivia4.htm: U.S. Constitution quiz for kids.

## TOWN MEETING

Students participate in a town-meeting role-playing situation designed to help them experience democracy in action.

Duration: 1 class period
Group Size: whole class
Disciplines: sociology, psychology, language arts, political science
Skills: evaluating, interpreting, analyzing, deducing, inferring

Key Vocabulary: vote, motion, second, town meeting, moderator, in favor of, not in favor of

Materials: writing materials

**Procedure**

1. Share with students how a town meeting works.
   a. Before meeting, the people of the town suggest ideas or topics they would like to see discussed and on which they will vote. A list of the ideas or topics is sent to every person in town who can vote. At the meeting, someone makes a motion to consider the first item from the list ("I move that we . . ."), and another person seconds it ("I second the motion."). The meeting can now discuss the motion. Voters speak for or against the motion.
   b. When everyone who wishes to speak has done so, the people vote on the idea. First the moderator calls for those in favor of the motion to raise their hands ("All those in favor of . . . , raise your hands"). Vote counters count the raised hands and record the number. The moderator then calls for those not in favor of the motion to raise their hands ("All those not in favor of . . . , raise your hands"). Vote counters count the raised hands and record the number. If more people vote for something than against it, the idea is passed.
2. Tell students that the class is going to have a town meeting, during which time they will be able to vote for or against an idea.
3. Identify a proposal or ask the class to think of some ideas, then narrow them to one item. Discuss what specific aspect of the item is to be discussed and generate a question regarding the item. (Examples: a new rule about how something is done in the classroom, playground, or cafeteria; the addition of a new game, procedure, or activity in the classroom or at recess; a special project to help the school or larger community such as cleaning up the playground, planting flowers, building bird feeders; recycling in the classroom).
4. Divide the class into groups and allow the groups to generate lists of arguments for and against the item.

5. Return to the whole-class setting. Select a moderator and choose one child to make the motion and another to second it. Preselect several children to make arguments for and against the motion, but also encourage unrehearsed opinions.
6. Before the meeting comes to order, discuss the rules that each person must follow:
   a. Raise your hand when you want to speak.
   b. Do not speak when someone else is talking.
   c. When the moderator calls on you, stand up, face the meeting, and say what you want to say.
   d. Always use polite language.
7. When the moderator calls for the vote, raise your hand to vote yes or no. Don't lower it until the vote counters have finished counting and have told you that your hand may be lowered.
8. When students are ready to vote, be sure they understand that they are voting yes if they raise their hands when the moderator asks, "All those in favor," and that they are voting no if they raise their hands when the moderator asks, "All those not in favor."

## Extensions/Adaptations

- Reconvene the meeting, perhaps on a monthly basis, to discuss other issues.
- Explain to the students that on some issues, people prefer to vote privately rather than publicly. In that case, the vote is done with paper ballots, either at the meeting or on a special voting day. Have children vote on an issue using paper ballots on which they write "yes" or "no." Have vote counters tally the votes and present the results on a chart or bar graph.
- Invite "the media" to "cover" the town meeting. Select several children to observe the meeting and present news stories on it. Interview different voters on how they feel about the town meeting.

## Recommended Children's Books

Barnes, Peter, & Barnes, Cheryl. (1999). *Woodrow for President*. Vacation Spot Publications.

Benson, Michael, et al. (2003). *True for Kids Readers: New England Town Meeting*. Harcourt Horizons.

Christelow, Eileen. (2003). *Vote!* Clarion Books.

Maestro, Betsy. (1998). *The New Americans: Colonial Times*. Harper Collins.

Maestro, Betsy. (1998). *Voice of the People: Democracy in Action*. Harper Trophy.

Peet, B. (1981). *The Wump World*. Houghton Mifflin.

### Technology Resources

www.sec.state.vt.us/Kids/kids_index.htm: Information and activities including town meetings for grades K–3.

www.eduplace.com/ss/act/meeting.html: Children experience democracy in action by taking part in a town meeting.

www.michigan.gov/scope/1,1607,7-155-10710_13476_13480-54379–,00 .html: A lesson featuring a town meeting in role-play for children.

## SCHOOL GROUNDS CLEAN-UP

By participating in a school grounds clean-up, students become aware of personal interactions with individuals and their environment in order to carry out relevant social action.

Duration: 1 class period

Group Size: whole class

Disciplines: sociology, language arts, ecology, science

Skills: observing, evaluating, interpreting, analyzing, deducing, inferring

Key Vocabulary: civic responsibility, recycle

Materials: materials as needed for clean-up efforts such as gloves, trash bags, paper towels, and glass cleaner; camera

### Procedure

1. As a class, identify an area of the school grounds that is important to the class. Determine what the class will accomplish in that location (pick up trash, remove weeds, add a coat of paint, plant

plants). Discuss safety issues (procedures for picking up sharp objects, etc.).

2. Collect supplies from the appropriate places within the school (gloves, trash bags, paper towels, and glass cleaner).

3. Take "before," "during," and "after" photos.

4. Collect two items of trash from each student and place in a garbage bag. Once in the classroom again, take out one piece at a time and have students categorize them into recycle or nonrecycle piles. Discuss the importance of recycling.

5. After the clean-up, discuss: Who did your clean-up help? What did you see and hear during the clean-up? How did the clean-up make you feel? What did you learn that you did not know before? What new questions or ideas do you have? Is there anything you would do differently the next time?

6. Using a photo from some aspect of the clean-up, have each student construct a journal entry about how the experience can make a person more aware of civic responsibility.

7. Write a class letter to your local newspaper and describe the project. Describe its importance and what other students can do to help take care of it. Send the "before" and "after" pictures with the letter.

## Extensions/Adaptations

- Go back to your area once a month to keep it clean.
- Identify waste issues that affect areas in the local community.
- Predict what would happen if waste was not disposed of appropriately.
- Develop and maintain a compost pile.

## Recommended Children's Books

Brown, Laurie, & Brown, Marc. (1994). *Dinosaurs to the Rescue*. Little, Brown and Company.

Kielburger, Marc, & Kielburger, Craig. (2002). *Take Action! A Guide to Active Citizenship*. Wiley Publishing.

Lewis, Barbara. (1992). *Kids with Courage*. Free Spirit Publishing.

Lewis, Barbara, & Espeland, Pamela. (1995). *The Kid's Guide to Service Projects*. Free Spirit Publishing.

Lewis, Barbara, Espeland, Pamela, & Perno, Caryn. (1998). *The Kid's Guide to Social Action*. Free Spirit Publishing.

Maze, Stephanie. (2000). *I Want to Be an Environmentalist*. Harcourt Brace Publishing.

Peet, B. (1981). *The Wump World*. Houghton Mifflin

Seuss, Dr. (1971). *The Lorax*. Random House.

## Technology Resources

www.pbs.org/democracy/kids/educators/citizenshipcity.html: Helping students visualize their town's government through activities.

www.crf-usa.org/network/net8_l: Fostering civic responsibility through service learning.

www.imakenews.com/psla/e_article000142184.cfm: Making civic responsibility a reality in the classroom.

# *Assessment and Evaluation*

Assessment involves the process of observing and accumulating objective evidence of an individual child's progress in learning. Authentic assessment consists of the examination of meaningful tasks; self-assessment; and application of concepts, skills, and knowledge. Evaluation involves interpreting the information gathered through means of assessment and of making final judgments about the effectiveness of teaching for learning. To effectively measure student achievement, a balanced assessment program must be implemented in the social studies curriculum. No single tool should be used to the exclusion of others; single tools cannot provide the quality of information needed to determine a student's knowledge of concepts; content integration; and acquisition of content skills, process skills, and lifelong learning skills.

Rubrics help implement a well-balanced assessment program by providing specified criteria for objective assessment that can be used as part of final-evaluation judgments. These scoring guides describe student work at differing levels of performance, provide students with feedback on performance, identify what is needed to achieve a certain score, and provide students the opportunity to specifically identify what is required and what areas need improvement. Rubrics can be developed to accommodate scoring using either specific (letter or number grades) or non-specific (unsatisfactory, needs improvement) assessment and evaluation. They also can be used as a teacher-directed or self-assessment instrument. A rubric's content consists of three components: (1) definitions of the knowledge and skills to be assessed, (2) a scale of possible points to be assigned for a given range, and (3) a description of each level of performance. These components should allow students to communicate their responses in a variety of ways, as long as the purposes of the assignment have been met. Following are sample rubrics that can be used for several activities in this book.

## DISCUSSION RUBRIC

The following is a group problem-solving and open-ended discussion-question rubric for oral responses or written problem solving.

**Exemplary: 4 points (A).** The responses clearly demonstrate complete understanding of the process involved and a clear, concise rationale for the solutions made.

**Competent: 3 points (B).** The responses generally present a solid understanding of the process involved, but a clear rationale for the solutions made was not identified.

**Satisfactory: 2 points (C).** The responses show an understanding of the process involved, but the solution itself is incomplete and the rationale is unclear.

**Inadequate: 1 point (D).** The responses do not show an understanding of the process involved by not being relevant to the problem under discussion.

**No Response: 0 points (F).**

## TABLE, GRAPH, OR CHART ACTIVITY RUBRICS

### Option 1

5. The chart gives a complete and understandable message; all rows and columns have clear headings and follow an identifiable pattern; measures used are indicated; the source of data is included in a footnote; all chart components are labeled; a title makes clear the information presented; the chart contains all pertinent information; and the end product is legible, neat, and conforms to a written standard.

4. The chart gives a complete and understandable message; all rows and columns have clear headings; measures used are indicated; the source of data is included; most chart components are labeled;

a title makes clear the information presented; the chart contains most pertinent information; and the end product is legible, neat, and conforms to a written standard. (Approximately 80 percent or more of the identified criteria).

3. The chart gives an understandable message; all rows and columns have clear headings; measures used are indicated; most chart components are labeled; a title is included; the chart contains pertinent information, but some omissions are evident; the end product is legible and neat and attempts to conform to a written standard. (Approximately 50 to 80 percent of the identified criteria).

2. The chart does not contain 50 percent of the identified criteria, contains significant errors, and/or is of poor quality related to legibility, neatness, and a written standard.

1. The chart was not completed and does not show comprehension of the subject/content.

0. No work was submitted.

## Option 2

The chart gives a complete and understandable message of the content being related. (Yes/No)

All rows and columns have headings that follow an identifiable pattern. (Yes/No)

The measure(s) used is(are) indicated. (Yes/No)

The source of the data is included in a footnote. (Yes/No)

The title makes clear what is being related. (Yes/No)

Legible handwriting is used. (Yes/No)

The chart is precise and easy to recognize. (Yes/No)

The chart contains no significant errors. (Yes/No)

The chart is well organized. (Yes/No)

The chart is complete. (Yes/No)

## GROUP-WORK RUBRIC

Identify points for each subheading. Average and indicate points on a line beside each heading. Determine final score by examining scale at bottom of rubric.

| | Always | Usually | Sometimes | Never |
|---|---|---|---|---|
| Participation in | | | | |
| All Tasks: _____ | | | | |
| performed assigned task | 1 | 2 | 3 | 4 |
| helped team members | 1 | 2 | 3 | 4 |
| contributed to the group | 1 | 2 | 3 | 4 |
| Time Use:_____ | | | | |
| stayed on task | 1 | 2 | 3 | 4 |
| monitored team activities | 1 | 2 | 3 | 4 |
| completed work promptly | 1 | 2 | 3 | 4 |
| Behavior:_____ | | | | |
| courteous to all | 1 | 2 | 3 | 4 |
| used appropriate language | 1 | 2 | 3 | 4 |
| was a "team player" | 1 | 2 | 3 | 4 |

Scale: 9–12 points (A); 13–18 points (B); 19–24 (C); 25 or more points indicates a need for improvement.

## RUBRIC FOR WRITTEN ASSIGNMENTS

All activities can be adapted to incorporate a writing component. The focus should be on process writing to include prewriting, drafting, revising, editing, and successful production of the final copy. A written response can be considered unscoreable for several reasons: unrelated to specified assignment, no response, illegible response, incomprehensible response, fraudulent, or response so incomplete that the reader cannot determine if the assignment was addressed.

### Option 1: Checklist Format

*Appropriate Grammar and Usage*

- ☐ sentence structure
- ☐ subject/verb agreement
- ☐ use of plurals
- ☐ pronoun agreement
- ☐ verb tense
- ☐ adjective/adverb use
- ☐ lack of sentence fragments
- ☐ lack of run-on sentences

*Appropriate Use of Mechanics*

- ☐ capital letters
- ☐ periods
- ☐ question marks
- ☐ colons
- ☐ commas
- ☐ apostrophes
- ☐ spelling

*Appropriate Organization*

- ☐ topic selection
- ☐ outline
- ☐ introduction
- ☐ topic sentences
- ☐ supporting sentences
- ☐ transitions
- ☐ paraphrasing
- ☐ conclusions

## Option 2: Scoring Method

*Focus*

To what extent does the written work present and maintain the main idea?

**6.** Focuses on topic; seems complete or whole.
**5.** Focuses primarily on topic, but has one or two unrelated ideas; seems complete or whole.
**4.** Generally focuses on topic but has several unrelated ideas; seems complete or whole.
**3.** Generally focuses on topic but has some unrelated ideas; no sense of completeness.
**2.** Slightly relates to topic; has irrelevant ideas.
**1.** Slightly addresses topic; has irrelevant ideas.

*Organization*

To what extent does the paper have a beginning, middle, and end? Are the points logically related to one another?

**6.** Has logical beginning, middle, and end; includes transitional words and phrases.

**5.** Has logical beginning, middle, and end; some transitional words and phrases used.

**4.** Beginning, middle, or end not clearly defined or logical; some transitional words and phrases included.

**3.** Beginning, middle, and/or end not defined or logical; little use of transitional words or phrases.

**2.** Beginning, middle, and end not clearly defined or logical; little use of transitional words or phrases.

**1.** Beginning, middle, and end not clearly defined or logical; no use of transitional words or phrases.

*Support*

To what extent do the supporting details used in the written work explain, clarify, or define? Are word choices accurate and specific?

**6.** Uses exemplary details—specific, credible, thorough; precision in word choice.

**5.** Uses adequate supporting ideas; adequate word choices, mainly precise.

**4.** Does not fully develop supporting ideas; adequate word choice, not always precise.

**3.** Provides some supporting ideas; some undeveloped ideas; adequate but imprecise word choices.

**2.** Develops supporting details inadequately or illogically; limited or immature word choice.

**1.** Lacks development of ideas; few supporting details; limited or immature word choice.

*Conventions*

To what extent does the written work employ correct capitalization, punctuation, and spelling? Is sentence-structure variety used? Are complete sentences used? Is correct grammar used?

6. Correct spelling, punctuation, and capitalization; varied sentence structure; complete sentences; parts of speech used correctly.

5. Mainly correct spelling, punctuation, and capitalization; varied sentence structure; usually complete sentences; parts of speech usually used correctly.

4. Awareness of correct spelling, punctuation, and capitalization; simple sentences but attempts to vary; usually complete sentences; parts of speech used adequately.

3. Awareness of correct spelling, punctuation, and capitalization; simple sentences and unvaried structure; complete sentences and fragments used; adequate parts of speech used.

2. Frequent errors in capitalization, punctuation, and spelling; simple sentences and unvaried structure; complete sentences and fragments used; parts of speech used inconsistently and incorrectly.

1. Many errors; spelling errors tend to obscure meaning; simple sentences and unvaried structure; complete sentences, fragments, and run-on sentences used; parts of speech used inconsistently and incorrectly.

**Option 3: Writing Assignment Rubric for Open-Ended Questions**

**Exemplary: 4 points.** The response clearly demonstrates complete understanding of important ideas and process, provides accurate rationale, and includes diagrams if needed. Free of mechanical errors, usage problems, and flaws in sentence/phrasing structure.

**Competent: 3 points.** The response generally presents a solid understanding of important ideas and processes but may have omitted one or more minor elements or ideas, or may have failed to provide a clear rationale. Relatively free of mechanical errors, usage problems, and flaws in sentence/phrasing structure.

**Average: 2 points.** The response shows understanding of part of the question or process, but it is slightly incomplete, and the rationale may be unclear. May have some mechanical errors, usage problems, and flaws in sentence/phrasing structure.

**Unsatisfactory: 1 point.** The response does not show an understanding of the question; words, drawings, and diagrams are not relevant to the problem. Consistent mechanical errors, usage problems, and flaws in sentence/phrasing structure.

**Inadequate: 0 points.** The response, drawings, diagrams, and so on do not address the question; severe mechanical errors, usage problems, and flaws in sentence/phrasing structure.

Content
   Definition of problem
   Descriptive details; pros/cons
   Diagrams/Drawings
Structure
   Topic sentence
   Logical detail sentences to support topic
   Transitions between beginning, middle, and end
   Logical sequence
   Definite beginning, middle, and end
Mechanics
   Sentence Structure (fragments, run-ons)
   Capitalization
   Punctuation
   Citations
Expression
   Spelling
   Legibility/Word processing
   Style (APA)
   Vocabulary
Work Habits
   4 points: Works independently; accepts and uses suggestions; meets all deadlines.
   3 points: Works independently and collaboratively; usually accepts and uses suggestions; meets all deadlines.
   2 points: Works collaboratively only; lacks focus on task; ignores most suggestions; meets some deadlines.
   1 point: Works collaboratively only; lacks focus; ignores all suggestions; misses deadlines.
   0 point: No work evident.

# Magazines, Periodicals, and Professional Organizations

## MAGAZINES FOR CHILDREN

*Calliope*, 30 Grove Street, Suite C, Peterborough, NH 03458

*Cobblestone*, 30 Grove Street, Suite C, Peterborough, NH 03458

*Cricket*, 315 Fifth Street, Box 300, Peru, IL 61354

*Faces*, 30 Grove Street, Peterborough, NH 03458

*Highlights for Children*, 2300 West 5th Avenue, Columbus, OH 43272

*Kids Discover*, 170 Fifth Avenue, 6th Floor, New York, NY 10010

*National Geographic World*, P.O. Box 63001, Tampa, FL 33660

*Ranger Rick*, National Wildlife Foundation, 11100 Wildlife Center Drive, Reston, VA 20190

*3–2–1 Contact*, P.O. Box 7690, Red Oak, IA 51591

*Zillions*, P.O. Box 54832, Boulder, CO 80322

## PERIODICALS FOR TEACHERS

*Childhood Education*, 11501 Georgia Avenue, Suite 312, Wheaton, MD 20902

*The Horn Book*, 11 Beacon Street, Suite 1000, Boston, MA 02108

*Language Arts*, 1111 Kenyon Rd., Urbana, IL 61801

*The Reading Teacher*, 800 Barksdale Road, P.O. Box 8139, Newark, DE 19714

*Science and Children*, 1201 16th Street NW, Washington, DC 20005

*Science Scope*, 1201 16th Street NW, Washington, DC 20005

*Social Studies and the Learner*, 3501 Newark Street NW, Washington, DC 20016

*Social Studies Education*, 3501 Newark Street NW, Washington, DC 20016

*Teaching Pre K–8*, 40 Richards Avenue, Norwalk, CT 06854

*The WEB, Wonderfully Exciting Books*, Ohio State University Reading Center, 200 Ramseyer Hall, Columbus, OH 43210

## PROFESSIONAL ORGANIZATIONS

American Educational Research Association (AERA), 1230 17th St. NW, Washington, DC 20036; www.aera.org

American Library Association (ALA), 50 East Huron, Chicago, IL 60611; www.ala.org

American Montessori Society, 150 Fifth Avenue, Suite 203, New York, NY 10011

Association for Childhood Education International (ACEI), 11501 Georgia Avenue, Suite 315, Wheaton, MD 20902; www.acei.org

Association for Supervision and Curriculum Development (ASCD), 1250 N. Pitt Street, Alexandria, VA 22314; www.ascd.org

Center for Civic Education, Douglas Fir Road, Calabasas, CA 91302

Children's Book Council, 568 Broadway, New York, NY 10012

Council for Basic Education, 725 15th Street NW, Washington, DC 20005

Council for Exceptional Children (CEC), 1920 Association Drive, Reston, VA 22091

International Reading Association (IRA), P.O. Box 8139, Newark, DE 19714; www.ira.org

International Technology Education Association, 1914 Association Drive, Reston, VA 22091

Junior Achievement, National Headquarters, One Education Way, Colorado Springs, CO 80906

Literacy Volunteers of America, 5795 Widewaters Parkway, Syracuse, NY 13214

National Alliance of Black School Educators, 2816 Georgia Avenue NW, Suite 4, Washington, DE 20001

National Association for Bilingual Education, 1220 L Street NW, Suite 605, Washington, DC 20005

National Association for the Education of Young Children (NAEYC), 1834 Connecticut Ave. NW, Washington, DC 20009; www.naeyc.org

National Association of Independent Schools, 75 Federal Street, 6th Floor, Boston, MA 02110

National Catholic Education Association, 1077 30th Street NW, Suite 100, Washington, DC 20007

National Congress of Parents and Teachers, 700 North Rush Street, Chicago, IL 60611

National Council for Geographic Education, Indiana University of PA, 16a Leonard Hall, Indiana, PA 15705; www.ncge.org

National Council for History Education, 26915 Westwood Road, Suite B-2, Westlake, OH 44145; www.history.org/nche

National Council for the Social Studies, 3501 Newark Street NW, Washington, DC 20016; www.ncss.org

National Council of Teachers of English, 1111 Kenyon Road, Urbana, IL 61801; www.ncte.org

National Council of Teachers of Mathematics, 1906 Association Drive, Reston, VA 22091; www.nctm.org

National Council on Economics Education, 1140 Avenue of the Americas, New York, NY 10036; 800-338-1192; www.nationalcouncil.org/

National Education Association, 1201 16th Street NW, Washington, DC 20036; www.nea.org

National Geographic Society, P.O. Box 63002, Tampa, FL 33663; www.nationalgeographic.com

National Home Education Network, P.O. Box 1652, Hobe Sound, FL 33475; www.nhen.org/

National Middle School Association, 4807 Evanswood Drive, Columbus, OH 43229; www.nmsa.org

National School Volunteer Program, 601 Wythe Street, Suite 2000, Alexandria, VA 22314

National Science Resources Center, National Academy of Sciences, Smithsonian Institute, P.O. Box 37012, Washington, DC 20013

National Science Teachers Association (NSTA), 1742 Connecticut Ave. NW, Washington, DC 20009; www.nsta.org

Project Learning Tree, 1111 19th St. NW, Suite 780, Washington, DC 20036; www.plt.org

Project WET; www.projectwet.org/

Project WILD, Council for Environmental Education, 5555 Morningside Drive, Suite 212, Houston, TX 77005; www.projectwild.org

Reading is Fundamental, 600 Maryland Avenue SW, Suite 500, Washington, DC 20024; www.rif.org/

Teachers of English to Speakers of Other Languages, 1600 Cameron Street, Suite 300, Alexandria, VA 22314; www.tesol.org

United States Department of Education, 400 Maryland Ave. SW, Washington, DC 20202; www.ed.gov/

# Background Information

## CHAPTER 1: WESTWARD EXPANSION AND DIVERSE CULTURES

As America first grew, the lands to the west were called territories. Initially, only Native Americans who were very few in number lived in the territories, but gradually, especially in the 1800s, people of many cultures living in the east moved west for a variety of reasons. For example, some were missionaries who wanted to convert the Native Americans to Christianity, some went in search of gold, some were looking for rich farmland, some African American families came seeking freedom both before and after the Civil War, some Chinese immigrants were brought in as labor or came looking to find work and riches, and yet others were looking for a place where they could worship freely. Regardless of the specific reason, all of these people were looking for a way they could improve their lives.

Generally, as people traveled across the plains, called the Great American Desert (although it was really a grassland prairie), their wagon trains would stop at towns west of the Mississippi River to purchase supplies needed for the trip. The purchases were added to the provisions that had been brought along by family members. Most of the supplies were for the trip and to help the pioneers settle their land when they arrived at their destination in the west.

Few of these pioneers thought of actually settling as they crossed the Great Plains on trails such as the Oregon Trail, the Santa Fe Trail, the Mormon Trail, the Sonora Trail, or the California Trail. However, they found that the Great Plains area was a good place to raise wheat, and the land was cheap.

Over the years, more and more pioneers traveling in wagon trains began to settle on the land that belonged to the Native Americans, whose people were eventually forced by the government to live on reservations. Eventually, and especially after the Civil War and the building of the transcontinental railroad, the west was populated with many farms, ranches, and towns. The people who formed these communities represented Jewish, Irish, Scottish, English, Chinese, African, German, Spanish, and many other cultures. When traveling west, many of these cultural groups traveled together and therefore ended up setting up small communities together.

## Chinese Heritage

For many Chinese, their cultural identity was very important to them, and they did not want to live anywhere but their homeland. Many Chinese, like other people, were going through hard times because there was no work and therefore little money with which to buy food. So, many unskilled laborers in China decided to leave China to find work in other countries. Some were tricked into leaving by labor recruiters who promised good pay and good working conditions in other parts of the world. Many Chinese men signed three-year labor contracts, thinking they could earn money to send back to help their families in China.

Many Chinese came to California and the west to work in mines when gold was discovered or to help build the railroads across the country. Those working on the railroad earned $1.00 per day, $.50 less than other workers. They were expected to pay for their own place to stay and their meals from their salary. One of the railroad jobs that had to be done was blasting pathways and tunnels through the tall, rugged Rocky Mountains. Many of the Chinese workers performed this demolition duty. To blast a hole in the side of a mountain, the worker was lowered by ropes in a large straw basket down the side of the mountain. The worker placed the charges in holes he drilled in the mountainside, lit the fuses, and was pulled back up by fellow workers before the charge exploded. Very often there were accidents that resulted in the workers being killed. The accidents were so numerous that the expression "Not even a Chinaman's chance" came into the American vernacular.

When the railroads quit hiring and let workers go, and when the Chinese left their jobs on their own, many returned to China. However, some remained in their new country and found other jobs. Some became vegetable farmers and grew many vegetables along the Santa Cruz River and sold them to people living nearby. Others found jobs as cooks and servants and eventually opened their own businesses, such as grocery stores, seamstress and tailoring shops, restaurants, and laundries. The Chinese were discriminated against, with many other cultures indicating resentment because the Chinese worked for such low wages. Laws were passed to keep the Chinese apart from other members of society and to make it difficult for new Chinese people to enter the country. This isolated the Chinese, and their small communities became even more important to them. In spite of this treatment, many Chinese chose to remain in the Southwest and become citizens. Today, Chinese communities are valued for their cultural contributions.

### Jewish Heritage

Although the west isn't widely known for its Jewish heritage, the Jewish population made several contributions. Generally, two primary waves of Jewish pioneers traveled to the west, the first with the opening of the Santa Fe Trail in 1821, and the next after the railroad was built in 1880.

Jewish pioneers were responsible for building the first railroad in Arizona, which ran between Clifton and Metcalf, Arizona. This was very difficult work, but the Jews saw the necessity of a railroad to enable easier access between the East and the West. Many were merchants and traders who established different types of general stores on Main Streets in cities and towns throughout the Southwest. Others worked the land as farmers and ranchers. Some who started out as cattle herders gradually progressed to shepherd, cattle tycoon, and finally sheep baron.

### African Americans

African Americans hold a very diversified place in the history of America's westward expansion. During the early and middle 1800s, several African Americans were explorers, fur trappers, scouts, and businessmen. Some were freed slaves brought to the country originally during the explorations of the Spanish.

As more and more people moved west, more and more slaves escaped into the northern states between the Sierra Madre mountains, while others went to Texas and Oklahoma. After emancipation and the Civil War, thousands went to work on ranches and rode the cattle trails northward. During this time, the U.S. Army was designated to keep peace and order in the region. About 20 percent of the troops were African American and came to be known as the Buffalo Soldiers.

Many African Americans became cowboys. They worked on ranches, herding and branding cattle, and riding the trails from Texas northward to grasslands on the plains. They experienced the same hardships as did all cowboys, and some were killed in stampedes, some froze or were overcome by the extreme summer temperatures, and some drowned. A large number remained on the northern plains, while others rode back south and stopped to settle in towns along the way.

**Hispanic Heritage**

The Hispanic settlers infused Hispanic customs, language, culture, and religion into the new territories. The Spanish possessed much of what is today the southwest United States. During the early exploration and colonization of lands west of the Mississippi, the Spanish were the main explorers and colonizers. Sent by the King of Spain and the Catholic Church, the conquistadors and the priests established a series of trails known as El Camino Real (The King's Highway), which connected a series of missions throughout the areas that became the southern United States and especially in the Southwest. Many of these missions formed the basis for cities that developed around them. In 1821, when Mexico declared independence from Spain, more Hispanic settlers already established in the East crossed the continent and continued the establishment of towns and villages. The most common form of transportation was the Spanish caretta. The carreta was a crudely constructed two-wheeled wagon with springless axles and peg construction that was pulled by oxen. This meant a very rough ride for anyone or anything in the wagon, although the trails on which the carreta was used were deeply grooved, which caused the large wheels to travel more smoothly. In addition to traveling long distances, the carreta was used by women to carry laundry to the river, as well as to haul wood, merchandise for trading, and supplies.

### Native American

The only indigenous people of the West were the Native Americans. There were many tribes that followed varied lifestyles, from the nomadic Plains Indians who relied mainly on buffalo hunting for their main sustenance to the agricultural Navajo who lived in permanent cities. In addition to the Indians who were native to the West, many members of the eastern tribes were forced west by the American government. The best-known example of the westward movement of the eastern tribes was the forced migration known as the Trail of Tears, when many of the Cherokee people were taken from the Appalachian Mountains and moved to Oklahoma.

The Native Americans did not give up their land easily. Against great odds, they fought bravely those who tried to take the land. Many were killed. Often they retreated, but at the first opportunity they would fight again for their lands. Many helped the Confederacy during the Civil War because they believed they would have a better chance of not being forced to give up their lands if the Confederacy won.

### CHAPTER 2: CONESTOGA WAGON INFORMATION

**History.** These wagons were built in Conestoga, Pennsylvania, in the mid-1700s. They were drawn by six or eight horses, mules, or oxen. Together, the animals and each wagon could stretch as far as 60 feet. This sturdy, colorful wagon, also called the prairie schooner or covered wagon, was used by American pioneers and could carry up to six tons of cargo and was usually used to carry furniture, clothes, food, chests, water, tools, and other important items a family would need on a long trip.

**Body.** Usually painted blue and red, the body had seams between boards that were stuffed with tar to prevent leaks when crossing rivers.

The Conestoga wagon was built to withstand all types of weather. Deep sides provided protection from bullets and arrows that very seldom proved to be a problem—contrary to many Western movies. Its height was up to 11 feet, its length was up to 24 feet, and its width was 5 to 6 feet.

**Wheels.** The wheels were up to six feet high so axles could get over stumps and ruts in the road. Oak rims were about 10 inches wide and reinforced with iron that helped prevent sinking in the mud. Wheels could be removed if broken, or removed so the wagon could be used as a boat, which is why the wooden body was canoe shaped.

**Cover.** White canvas was stretched over the 8 to 12 bows of wood. This provided for privacy and for protection from the weather.

**Tongue.** This was a wooden pole that extended from the front of the wagon out to the length of one horse and assisted in steering the wagon.

**Barrel.** This was necessary for water storage for human and animal consumption.

**Lazy Board.** This was an oak board that projected from the side of the wagon where the driver sat or stood to guide the animals and operate the wagon.

**Feed Box.** This was a bucket or box at the back of the wagon for feeding the animals.

**Brake.** This was located against the left rear wheel and was operated by a lever and rope.

**Tool Chest.** This was located beside the water barrel and contained tools necessary for making wagon repairs during the trip.

## CHAPTER 2: THE AMERICAN COWBOY

The role and responsibilities of the American cowboy, along with his clothes and equipment, have a long history that began in the early 1800s with the Mexican vaqueros. Cowboys were of many nationalities, mostly American, but also Mexican, Irish, German, English, and others. Many had formerly been soldiers in the Confederate and Union armies, but some were young men, often 16 or 17 years old, who were seeking adventure. Some were older men who wanted to move away from the crowded cities in the East. Others had become tired of farming or mining and wanted to try a new way of life. Still others were from places where they had difficulty with the law and wanted to start a "new life." Recently freed African Americans were also attracted to life in the West where they were judged by their work rather than by the color of their skin. But no matter what his background, each cowboy was responsible for the job assigned to him and had to work cooperatively with the other cowboys as a team. If they were not willing to do this, they lost their jobs and had to leave.

The cowboys learned their job from the Mexican vaqueros who had been herding wild cattle found in the Southwest. From these vaqueros, the cowboys learned to rope, brand, and herd cattle. They also adopted the kind of equipment and clothing useful and necessary in doing their jobs and often improved upon these elements. They used wide-brimmed hats, bandannas, flap pockets, high boots with pointed toes and high insteps, a rolled slicker, leather chaps, saddles and saddle horns, gloves with coves, and rope.

## CHAPTER 8: BACKGROUND ON FINGERPRINTING

Fingerprints have been used as a means of identification for centuries. In ancient Babylon, fingerprints were used on clay tablets for business transactions, and thumbprints have been found on clay seals in ancient China. In 1903, fingerprints were first used in the United States by the New York prison system. The first criminal conviction based on fingerprint evidence was the case of Thomas Jennings, who committed a burglary in 1911.

Fingerprints offer a means of personal identification. The outer layer of skin on fingers is made up of a series of ridges. The ridges on each person's fingers are unique. While some personal characteristics can change (such as hair color and length), fingerprints do not. Almost every time a person touches something, a fingerprint is left on the object. Hands are covered with sweat pores. Sweat is often mixed with other body oils and dirt, and when something is touched with a person's fingers, the oils and dirt on the skin stick to the surface of the object leaving an imprint of the person's fingertips.

There are three kinds of prints. Prints that can be seen with the naked eye are called visible prints; invisible prints are the most common kind of prints and are called latent prints; a print that leaves an impression on such objects as soap or clay is called a plastic print. People who are trained in using fingerprints as a means of identification to help solve crimes are known as forensic scientists. The FBI has a collection of millions of fingerprints. Investigators often compare fingerprints from a crime scene to the fingerprints in the FBI fingerprint bank (which is on computer) to see if they can find a match and thus know who committed the crime. They often fingerprint suspects to see if their fingerprints match those found at the crime scene.

There are three basic types of fingerprints: the arch, the whorl, and the loop. Arch patterns have lines that start at one side of the print and then rise toward the center of the print and leave on the other side of the print. Whorl patterns have a lot of circles that do not leave either side of the print. Loop patterns have lines that start on one side of the print and then rise toward the center of the print and leave on the same side of the print from which they started.

**Leslie Marlow** (Ed.D.) and **Duane Inman** (Ph.D.) are professors of education at Berry College, where they teach in the Charter School of Education and Human Sciences. They have authored numerous articles related to integrated teaching methodology; developed and presented workshops for public school systems, resource teachers, and other professionals; implemented mini-courses and workshops for teacher certification and in-service; and presented research and activities at international, national, regional, and state conferences. They have also worked extensively with public schools involved in curricular design and school improvement. Each was awarded the designation of distinguished educator by the state of Tennessee. Most recently they have completed a set of reading/language arts skill books and instructional materials (EduStrands, EduPaks, EduKey, and EduTests), coauthored with Dr. Ben Barron.

Dr. Marlow received her Ed.D. from the University of Alabama in curriculum and instruction with emphasis in social studies, reading, and language arts. She has worked as an early childhood and elementary school classroom teacher, teacher educator, and children's museum program director. Dr. Inman received his Ph.D. from the University of South Florida in science education. He has taught in public and private middle and secondary schools, worked as a teacher educator, served as an educational products manager within the private sector, and currently serves as chair of teacher education at Berry.